THE STRAW THAT FIXED THE CAMEL'S BACK

THE STRAW THAT FIXED THE CAMEL'S BACK

by

PETER HEREDIA & DAVID WILD

ISBN: 978-9948-799-16-0 (paperback)

Contents

Introduction

Do we need another book about selling? Yes. It's time to get back to basics. Over the years, the art of sales and selling has become overly elaborate, and the fundamentals of selling have become hidden behind the dazzle of polished complexity.

This book aims to rediscover the art of selling, and to demonstrate that there's not one single magic solution that will solve all your selling problems. Instead, success happens when you do more of the right things well, and less of the wrong things. Success happens when you pay attention to the fundamentals of sales and put them into practice in a systematic way. It's not rocket science. But it does take effort and application.

If you're up for the challenge, dive right in.

Who this book is for

We've written this book for anyone who wants to get better at selling. So, this book is for you if you're:

An experienced sales professional and feel you need a tune up, or you're not getting the results you want, and you want to know why. Or you may not even realise you're slipping. In many jobs, if you make a mistake or need improvement, your boss or colleague will point it out. But nearly all of the mistakes a salesperson makes are in front of someone who rarely provides feedback – the customer. So you may be blissfully unaware of bad habits, picked up over the years, that are holding you back.

New into sales, with little or no experience, and you'd feel more confident with a comprehensive grounding in the art of selling.

A small business owner who isn't a sales professional but would like to apply sales principles to grow a business

A sales manager with a sales team to manage.

We hope that anyone, whatever their level of sales experience or knowledge, will find new, unknown or half-forgotten skills, knowledge and attitudes that will skyrocket their results.

What we hope you'll get out of this book

This book will help you **do more of the right things more often and better**. It will help bring the right sales activities into your day-to-day sales life. It's packed with information and tips that make up an effective sales practice.

We see success in sales as a balancing act – the more positive sales behaviours you practise, the higher your chances of success. We can't tell you which particular sales fundamentals will make you the most successful. As you practise more techniques, something will tip the balance towards making a great sale – but what tips that balance will depend on the customer and your own approach. But there's nothing complicated here. Just keep loading the balance and it will eventually swing in your favour.

We're confident that by the end of the book you'll be:

- Doing more of the right sales activities.
- Doing the right sales activities better.
- Increasing your sales.

Who we are

We're Peter Heredia and David Wild. Between us, we've more than 70 years of selling successfully, and we still love what we do. That's because selling is such a crazy, varied, fascinating way of being. We must think on our feet and constantly make on-the-spot decisions. We answer to many masters – our customers, our own organisations, our boss. No two situations are the same. And there's a lot at stake – if we suck at our job, profits drop and so do our salaries and bonuses. Managing it all is complex but fun.

We also love selling because it stretches us. It develops a whole range of skills and intelligences, such as:

- Emotional intelligence: we're dealing with people every day.
- Strategic thinking: long term planning for long term gains.
- Structure: doing **all** the things that matter, not just the fun things.
- Resilience: making that round of sales calls when you're just not in the mood and you've had your ninth rejection of the day.

Why the title?

We had a good think about the title. Being successful in sales isn't about the quick fix, the magic bullet, the do-this-one-thing-and-you'll-succeed. It's about building a skills base, creating a toolbox of sales skills to learn and practise everyday.

"The straw that broke the camel's back" is a phrase we've all heard, and it resonated with us. That straw – that final, tiny object – is the thing that finally incapacitates that poor proverbial camel. That straw is just the last of many straws, of many burdens.

But what if we turned it around? What is that one tiny thing, on top of other tiny things, that can fix something that's broken? If your sales results aren't as good as you'd hoped for, this book will give you a range of ways to improve. As you put more skills into practice, the more straws you load up, your sales will become stronger and stronger until, one day, you'll fix it.

How to use this book:

For each chapter, we:

- Explain what the chapter's about.
- Explain why the topic is integral to the sales process.
- Explain the activities and skills you'll need to be successful.
- Give you some tips to get started: the 'straws'

We've designed each chapter to be a standalone guide to each aspect so you're welcome to dip into each or any of the chapters, or read it the whole way through from start to finish.

We firmly believe that the better you get at selling, the more you'll love it. We hope that it brings you a long and rewarding career, like the ones we've enjoyed over so many decades.

Look out for rainmaking activities

A rainmaking activity is fertiliser for your sales success. This is an activity that doesn't seem to be doing much, but in the background it's strengthening and enriching your sales process for bigger results in the future.

How to feel better about rainmaking activities

Salespeople love making sales so it's easy just to do the stuff that's clearly linked to making those sales – things like going to see a client or closing business. Rainmaking activities aren't always linked clearly to getting in that revenue. For instance, when you've had a morning of sales calls (rainmakers!) and everyone's told you, "No thanks," it's hard to feel great about it. So, to feel better, why not link those rainmaking activities to revenue? Here's an example:

Let's say you make 50 prospective phone calls. Out of these, you get 10 meetings (well done you!). Out of these 10 meetings you win two deals, worth $5,000 each (double well done you!). Take that 10K, divide it by your 50 calls, and you'll find each of your calls is worth $200 each.

Psychologically, showing yourself that each call makes money can be a bit of a motivator for those rainmaking activities.

Rainmaking activities are things like:

- Your Power Hour.
- Nurturing your existing client base.
- Meeting and developing new contacts.

CHAPTER 1:
Your Way of Selling

What's this about?

This section is about the importance of developing and designing your own individual way of selling. It shows you why it's important, and some of the constituent parts of a sales process to get you started.

Selling can be a complex process, if you let it. There are lots of constituent parts, stages and skills that go into the process of making a sale. So the one thing you can do to simplify sales for your business is to decide what your sales process is going to be.

This is called developing your Way of Selling.

The Way of Selling

It may sound a bit Zen, but by deciding, creating and developing a single source of truth for everything sales in your company, you'll make life easier and sales bigger.

It doesn't matter if it's just you selling stuff or you manage a small sales team or you have responsibility for a whole network of sales agents around the globe.

It's your way of selling, so name it. Your company is called Fuzzy BobChunks? You now have a process called "The Fuzzy BobChunks Way of Selling." Congratulations.

Giving it a name makes it a 'thing' in your organisation.

Having your Way of Selling is one of the most important foundations of sales success.

Here's why:

Clarity

A sales process is a clear and understood way in which your company sells its stuff. Note the two magic words: Clear. Understood.

When a sales process is articulated, set out, explained, made clear to all the people selling, everyone is working from the same process. There's no time or brains wasted in trying to work out, "What do I do next?".

There's no confusion. Just the next right step to take.

Now, this doesn't mean you'll all become Stepford sales people. There's lots of room for personality and independence within a Way of Selling. But having an agreed process helps everyone become successful.

Focussed activity

You should be able to reduce your company's Way of Selling down into a one-page document or browser screen. Keep it in front of mind, visible and easy on the eye to review. A salesperson should be able to look at it daily and be reminded to action all of the key activities that they should be completing every day. For example, it reminds them if they need to:

- Make more visits to their existing clients.
- Spend time looking for new opportunities.
- Unclog their pipeline (sounds gross but it's not what you think. All will be revealed later).

Without a focus, we've found that it can be easy for salespeople to drift into autopilot and end the day without making much progress on any front. If you've ever had the feeling when you're driving home that you've been busy all day but not really achieved much — and certainly made no sales — it's probably a distraction problem. There's so much busywork — but it's not the right work. Without a focus, it's easy to get lost in big picture activities, rather than what's helping you get to your target today. Keeping focussed on the right activities is key, so a daily, honest review of your one-page sale process helps you keep on track.

Your superpower: focus

Did we already mention focus? You bet we did. That's because in our experience, it's not that salespeople need to be more convincing, better listeners, better closers or more productive. What lets most salespeople down is that they're not focused enough. They don't do the stuff they need every day to enable them to hit their targets. And it's a lack of focus that causes this.

We know, because we've been there ourselves. It's just too easy for any salesperson to switch on cruise control and just do the job. Waking up every day, going to the office, making some calls and visits and then, fingers' crossed, achieving their sales targets. It's too easy, because selling is very much like spinning plates – there are lots of activities, and spending too much time spinning a particular plate means the others will fall. Having focus means being systematic in keeping to every element of the sales process: focussing on each task at the right time.

A lack of focus looks like this:

- Too much time on admin and not enough focus on making calls to plan the week ahead.
- Too much time on closing deals and not enough focus on adding opportunities to the pipeline.

- Too much time looking for new business and not enough focus on existing customers.
- Too much time on customers that demand attention and not enough focus on the customers that don't demand attention but should be getting it anyway *(Note from Peter: "I lost my first ever customer because I lacked focus here." Sad face.)*

Bigger impact on sales

These 'right' activities that you're now enthusiastically focussed on – these are 'right' activities because they are Revenue Generating Activities (RGA): things you do that get you closer to your goal of making more sales. If you have a more focussed approach, you'll do more RGAs and naturally increase your sales. It's just (very rough) maths. A brief daily review of your Way of Selling impacts the numbers. If you're spending 35% of your time on RGAs, and then you start your daily review of your Way of Selling, you might increase your RGA time by 5% to 40%. 5% is a good start, so don't mock. Down the line, you'll increase your revenue by the same uplift.

Improved efficiency and effectiveness

Your daily review of your Way of Selling helps you become more effective and efficient with your time and headspace. You'll get more out of your work day, however many hours you usually work. This is why:

- You're doing more of the RGAs and less of the woffly stuff.
- You'll get more skilled at doing the RGAs. As you practise doing them, you'll get better at them. It'll save you time and headspace.
- Yes, you'll be working smarter rather than harder. A trite phrase, yes, but it's trite because it's true.

Better opportunity management

Ok, buckle up, because we're going to talk a lot about opportunity management and the mysterious opportunity pipeline later.

It's not good opportunity management to have one huge (metaphorical) bucket, put every opportunity in there, peer into it and think, "What am I going to do with these?". Your Way of Selling gives you the direction to organise them: you'll know where in the process each opportunity is. Everything will have its place, and this means you'll know exactly what you're supposed to be doing (or not doing) with each opportunity, and when.

It's measurable

What gets measured gets done. We all know this, but usually, the only thing that gets measured in sales is revenue. Yep, this is so important for our success because we need to pay the wages, make a profit etc. But revenue is only the result of our RGAs. If we measure our RGAs, too, we'll have a truckload more information about whether we'll hit our revenue targets, and which RGA we may be missing.

Developing your Way of Selling

Your Way Of Selling is a process. It has a direction of travel and a set of activities for each stage of the process. It sounds prescriptive, and to an extent it is, as any process is. It keeps salespeople focussed on the next right activity, but there's room for personality within the process.

What's included in your Way of Selling?

Glad you asked. We talked earlier about Revenue Generating Activities (RGAs), remember? Well, your Way of Selling is a process that's made up of RGAs. Here's our Big Fat List of the RGAs that we think every Way of Selling should include, and is what we'll be covering in the rest of the book.

Big Fat List of RGAs

- Finding and managing potential customers
  - Identifying your target market
  - Building your target market
  - Understanding opportunities
  - Creating, feeding and managing an opportunity pipeline
  - Qualifying opportunities
  - Finding out if your pipeline is working

  - Keeping the momentum or following up
- Approaching potential customers
  - Identifying decision makers
- First meetings
  - Getting a first meeting
  - Preparing for a first meeting
  - Making a good first impression
  - Building rapport
  - Understanding your customer
  - Identifying their needs
- Developing a persuasive sales statement
  - Understanding features, advantages and benefits
- How to make offers
  - Quotes v proposals
  - In person v not in person
  - Presenting your solution
  - Handling objections
  - Negotiating
  - Closing business
- Managing and selling to existing customers

Now, you might be thinking, "If Our Way of Selling has all these RGAs in, then isn't this everyone's way of selling? We won't be any different from any other business. Boo hoo."

Let's clear this one up. Your Way of Selling will contain all these RGAs (because that's how you make sales) but you'll be making all the decisions that make your Way of Selling your own. You'll decide things such as:

- Your target market parameters.

- How long you want opportunities to stay in your opportunity pipeline.
- How you'll qualify leads.
- How you'll keep clients warm.

You'll make all the decisions about the numbers, performance indicators, targets, when you'll do what to whom and why. You'll take the bare bones of the Way of Selling (the RGAs) and dress it up as your own.

Some straws: The Way of Selling

- As you go through this book, build your Way of Selling.
- Make your Way of Selling easily accessible. Put it on a chart on the wall or a screen saver. It needs to be handy as you'll use it every day.
- Build your Way of Selling and review it every 3 – 6 months.
- Look at it for 15 or 20 seconds every day. That's it.

CHAPTER 2:
Doing the right things

What's this about?

This section's about managing your time, energy and head-space to make sure that you're focusing on the things that will get you to where you want to be – more sales without losing your sanity.

Why is it important?

When you're doing the right things in the right way, you can't help but increase your productivity and results. Yes, doing the right things means working smarter, not harder. (Trite, but true.)

In this section you'll find out the importance of:

- Good time management.
- The importance of focus.
- The Power Hour.

- Using methods of communication effectively.
- Setting reasonable targets for productive sales visits.

Managing your time correctly

Just as with any other job, managing our time properly is the key to achieving our goals, which in sales is usually making more sales. Managing our time well, with the right focus and maintaining a proactive attitude, is a rainmaking activity.

When we're in sales (or any job, really), it's easy to drift. When we're neck deep in daily activities, office politics and admin, it's easy to lose focus on our goal – making more sales (remember?). This could mean that we spend a lot of time:

- Working just on the things we like doing, and avoiding things we find difficult or are outside our comfort zone.
- Working only on the things we're measured on.
- Working on things because they've become routine and it's what everyone else is doing.
- Fire-fighting.

So, how do we handle our time to make our goal happen?

The answer is: The Power Hour.

The Power Hour

Your mission is to grab one hour every day to plan.

This is your Power Hour.

OK. It could be a Power Half Hour. Or a Power Twenty Minutes. But Power Hour sounds way cooler. The big takeaway is that you need to spend some time every day doing the powerful things that will make a massive difference to your sales success (in a good way).

We'll call it the Power Hour for now. You know what we mean.

Yes, we know that when you're not seeing clients, or if you're not working from home, you're back at the office doing the admin, writing up reports, solving little problems and, worst case scenario, stuck in meetings that have no purpose. Then there are the distractions: emails pinging and colleagues wanting a chat. It's so much easier to focus on work that comes to you than to be proactive with tasks that'll really up your sales. You will naturally respond to emails, you'll manage the request that just came in from the last phone call, you'll agree to do what your colleague has just asked you. All important things? Maybe. Maybe not. But none of these activities will drive more revenue in the future than what you do in your Power Hour, so it's important to grab one hour everyday.

What to do in your Power Hour

It's simple, really. Spend your Power Hour planning your days in the field i.e. planning how to get in front of, or to talk to clients or potential clients. When you're planning your meetings and calls with the appropriate opportunities and people you should be meeting, you're filling up your future sales.

We've found that the biggest barrier that prevents salespeople from ensuring they have as many meetings as possible with the right clients is finding the time to plan for it. Planning makes it happen.

Yes, but it's easy for you to say that. You don't work in my office!

We get it. Office life is one big carnival. How should we cope with distractions in real life, to enable us to grab that Power Hour? We've found that having a proactive policy for each of the three types of in-office distraction has helped us grab that uninterrupted time.

Here's how:

Distraction no 1: Colleagues

Yes, we love our colleagues but they're so distracting. They might have a relevant or urgent question, or they're passing by and think, "Oh, it's Pete, I need to talk to him about that thing," or they just want a chat.

Solution 1: A physical barrier

Find an office to lock yourself away. Or announce to your colleagues "Every day between 2pm and 3pm I will be in the coffee shop over the road doing my Power Hour. Do not come find me or I will end you." You probably shouldn't say that last sentence, no matter how tempting. You might start a Power Hour trend, though!

Solution 2: Introduce it to team culture

If you're a sales team leader, this is easy. During a team meeting, introduce the concept of the Power Hour and how it will benefit sales. Ask everyone to trial it for three months. Make it part of your team culture.

If you're not a team leader, suggest the Power Hour to your team leader, or bring it up in a team meeting. Tell your team members you're trialling it so you won't be available between 2pm and 3pm (or whatever time you decide, or ask the team when it is good for them not to disturb you). If you can't wait for the meeting, email your team that this is what you're trying out. It's polite to prepare people.

Solution 3: A psychological barrier

- Put headphones on at your desk. People are polite and will think twice about interrupting.
- Put a polite sign up at your desk asking for an interruption-free time, e.g. "Working on strategy between

2pm and 3pm. Please don't disturb me. Happy to chat outside this time. Thank you."

Distraction No 2: Emails and text messages

Checking for emails that 'might' have come in or "could be urgent" is just a habit. We've been trained like Pavlov's dogs to come to the call of any notification or automatically pick up our phone every two minutes to see if anything new has come up.

Solution: Here's how to eliminate email and text message distractions. It's easy:

- Turn your email/notifications/phone off for your Power Hour.
- Schedule a time to answer your emails and text messages.
- Don't have your email open 24/7. It's a good habit to get into.

Any properly urgent email can wait an hour. It just can. If your office is on fire, you won't get an email about it, so don't worry.

Distraction No. 3: Incoming phone calls

We've found that most salespeople love the phone, but don't take that love too far. You're not available 24/7, and especially not during your Power Hour.

Solution: Choose your favourite

- Set your mobile phone to silent mode so you won't be tempted to answer it.
- Heard of voicemail? Put your phone to voicemail, but make sure your voicemail message reassures the caller you'll get back to them within a set time frame.
- If you use a landline, redirect your landline to a colleague, who should field your calls and confirm that you'll get back to them after 60 minutes. Only ask to be contacted if there is an emergency and the caller truly cannot wait for a call back. You'll find there will not be many of these types of calls. You can return the favour when your colleague is working on their own Power Hour.

Using methods of communication effectively

Everyday you'll use email, messaging, the phone, video calls or in-person meetings to communicate aspects of your role as salesperson. Part of managing your time well is to understand which method of communication is most effective to use for which tasks.

Effective communication

There has been loads of research on what makes communication most effective (i.e. your meaning is received loud and clear just how you intended it), and one of the most understood is Albert Mehrabian's work. This quantifies how much of meaning is communicated via words, tone, and body language and suggests that:

- 7% of meaning is communicated through the spoken word.
- 38% is communicated through tone of voice.
- 55% is communicated through body language.

This ratio relates to in-person communication. But let's look at how we as salespeople communicate with customers. Our most common activities are:

- Email and other text messages.
- Phone calls.
- In-person meetings.

If we link the two together in a kind-of-loose way, how effective are our methods at communicating our meaning?

- Email (or other written message): 7%, as they're just getting the words and perhaps a little tone, but not much more.
- Phone calls: 45%, as they're getting words and tone.
- Meetings: 100%, as they're getting all three.

So, to be effective and efficient with our communication methods, when should we choose to use email, phone calls and in-person meetings?

Here's our take. Emails are effective for:

- Confirming something with a client or colleague: a meeting date, a fact, etc.
- Summarising an earlier meeting with a client, underlining action points and the steps ahead.

Phone calls are effective for:

- Warming up clients or thanking them.
- Reconfirming facts or double-checking.
- Asking a quick question.

In-person meetings are effective for:

- Understanding your client.
- Telling your client something new about what you can offer.
- Presenting your sales offer.

About sales visit targets

If you're using your Power Hour, you'll be getting in front of potential customers a lot more. So, should you set yourself sales visit targets?

Some companies continually push for their salespeople to make as many visits as is physically possible each day. Others don't have sales visit targets, but ask that their salespeople be productive in what they do, whatever that means to them.

To be successful, you need a bit of both. Balance is key.

If you're a sales team leader, you might push for strict visit targets because you're thinking "What gets measured gets done."

Here's why it doesn't work: If a salesperson is measured purely by high visit targets (which are most likely unachievable), they'll do their best to meet the target, even if it means manipulating what they are able to achieve, or attending lots of low-value but easy-to-arrange visits. Will this lead to overall success in their role as a professional salesperson, or the team leader's success? Or more sales? Probably not.

"Unachievable visit targets are bad" Story 1: Peter's the Rookie's Story:

In my first sales role out on the road, in the time before email, I was targeted to complete eight visits per day. The role also came with lots of administration, customer service issues and making formal proposals, too. I wanted to be successful but also wanted to hit the visit target, which was a very visible measure of performance.

After a few months I knew that I could make four scheduled visits on a daily basis, but there was just no time to do much else. So, for the other four, to 'tick the box' to ensure I hit my target, I would do anything the client asked for me to do that could somehow involve visiting their company. I would drop off supplies, packaging, invoices, promotional material at their reception, say hi to the receptionist while I was there and tick off that as a visit. It would have been easy for me to send stuff rather than visit and in many instances the visits achieved nothing.

I look back now and instead of manipulating the eight visits a day, I could easily have made one more scheduled visit. The four scheduled visits with solid objectives were making me successful, but the four 'drop in' visits helped me achieve my targets but achieved no extra sales. If I had not needed to worry about reaching the eight visits. I could easily have made one more scheduled visit to a real sales lead every day. That is 20% extra productivity!

"Unachievable visit targets are bad" Story 2: Business Cards Are Not A KPI

"The Managing Director of a printing cartridge company proudly told me that his salespeople made 20 visits per day. I was blown away, but I also found it extremely hard to believe. How was he measuring success? He pulled out a huge pile of business cards, which he put in front of me and said, "These were yesterday's visits". He expected his sales team to come back with 20 business cards each and every day to confirm that they had made 20 visits.

I asked if I could look at the business cards so I could understand more, and found a business card for a local butcher Now considering that their business was related to printing cartridges, seeing a card for a local butcher raised an eyebrow or three. I asked him to explain what a local butcher's requirements for printing cartridges would be, and he struggled. This wasn't an isolated card. More than half of the cards were for small businesses that would never fit their target audience. Clearly the sales team sold to their true target customers and went from door to door collecting any business card to make up their quota. And who could blame them?"

The moral of these stories is that unrealistic expectations for sales visit numbers defeat the purpose of making more sales.

But what if you have no visit targets?

Having looked at sales teams with extremely strict, often too high visit targets, let's go to the other extreme where there are no, or extremely low targets, in place for visiting clients. In our experience, we've noted that salespeople in companies with no visit targets tend to be unproductive, normally drifting along, doing admin, and lacking overall focus.

Let's say a company has a visit target of four a week. Say one visit takes an hour, plus one hour of travelling time — that's one full day to complete the 4 visits, or, with a bit more slack, let's say two full days to complete four visits. This means our mythical sales people would be sitting in the office for 3 or 4 days per week.

The key to success: Visits with an objective

Visit targets that are too high can lead to manipulation and less sales. Too low visit targets can lead to drifting and less sales. The key is to set a visit target for **meetings with a clear objective** that will contribute to generating sales: a productive visit. This will not only solve the too many/too few visit target dilemma, but also help you make sure you're directing all your visits to the goal of extra revenue.

So, which objectives make a productive meeting?

We've found that meetings with the following objectives contribute to sales growth:

- A first meeting with a client.
- Understanding the client and their needs.
- Educating the client: perhaps you have a new solution for them.
- Presenting your sales offer.
- Closing a deal.
- Negotiating.

Having an understanding of revenue-generating objectives will help you do more of the right thing. If you're a team leader, you can specify the types of visits that actually count for targets.

How to set a visit target for your team

For the most part, a salesperson's job is to be in front of a client so remove as much as possible of anything else that your team has to do. Focus effort on productive customer visits, but there's often a genuine need to spend up to half the day in the office.

So:

1. Decide on the office-based activities and how long these should take. Realistically.
2. Calculate how much time this leaves your team to spend on visits.
3. Calculate how many visits with a clear objective they can complete each day.
4. Once you arrive at each individual visit target, you can then consider the objectives from these visits. Once you understand this you can calculate if the number of objectives that are being met each week will be enough to hit their target.

If all your salespeople are achieving their visit targets, and every visit is delivering against the set objectives and you are still not achieving your revenue target, then you might need additional sales resources.

Don't forget that the number of productive visits a salesperson completes on the road is directly linked to their planning during their Power Hour.

Some straws: Doing the right things

- Don't forget your Power Hour.
- Make sure your visit targets are realistic.
- Make sure every visit has an objective.

CHAPTER 3:

Finding and managing opportunities

What's this about?

In this section you'll find out how to identify and select sales opportunities. It's a big world out there, and there are loads of businesses to sell to. How can you narrow the field so that you're only working on sales opportunities that you have more chance of winning?

You'll learn more about your target market, what opportunities are, the different types of opportunities, and why your opportunity pipeline is your new best friend.

Who's your customer?

Anyone who buys your product must have a reason. They must need what you can supply. Something has motivated them to have a requirement for what you can offer. If you clearly understand what the motivation is, you'll identify your customer and then define and build your target market accurately.

Total available market

Who in the world could possibly need your stuff? What would they use it for? When would they need it? What kinds of businesses need it more than others? How does it help them?

Now you've thought through who your customer is, you've identified your **total available market:** every possible business or individuals who may have a need for your product or service.

Target market

From your total available market, you'll identify your **target market**. This is made up of the businesses who you consider most likely to buy what you're selling. You'll focus your sales activity on your target market.

It's important to identify your target market. Not just because you'll have a better chance of selling, if they're more likely to buy, but you won't waste your time and effort on business opportunities that won't go anywhere.

It's also important to remember that, although the task of identifying your target market seems so far away from making a sale, it's the number one influencer in affecting your closing ratio.

What's a closing ratio?

A closing ratio is the percentage of deals you win against all the deals you try to make. For example, if you are trying to sell to 10 clients, and 4 of the ten buy what you're selling, your closing ratio is 40%. Well done you!

A well-selected target market means a higher closing ratio.

It's also important to understand that not everybody who needs or could use your product or service is your target market, and this will naturally become more and more apparent to you over time.

Peter's Story

Many years ago, I was crossing a bridge in town for a business meeting with a prospect. I suddenly realised that I only ever crossed this bridge to meet with prospects, never to meet with existing customers. I came to the conclusion that my target market simply didn't fit for that part of town. I had lost so much time attending these meetings over the years. I decided to rule out that part of town as a potential target market. It gave me more time to focus on my actual target market, and to close more deals with them.

Identifying and building your target market

Your target market is a subset of your total available market, so your next step is to identify it. Do this by extracting from the total available market the types and identities of businesses who are more likely to buy from you, and list them out. This is identifying and building a target market.

These businesses, the ones you've identified, could be actual businesses (e.g. FuzzyBobChunks Co Ltd) or types of businesses (e.g. restaurants).

Identifying your target market is a **rainmaking activity**. So, how do you identify and build your target market?

Ways to identify your target market 1: Market segmentation

Segmentation means breaking down your total available market into groups that mean something to your business. The objective is then to identify the groups that are most likely to buy your product or services.

There are lots of software tools that can help with this process, but, in our experience, it's the companies that take the time to think it through that are most successful.

Here are some common ways to segment your market:

- By industry: certain industries may need your product more than others.
- By location: maybe you can sell into some countries, but not others. Perhaps some places have more demand for what you're offering than others. Perhaps they have

offices internationally and to sell into that would your business strategy.

- By age of business: your product might be more suitable for long-term businesses or for start-ups.
- By size (employees): If your product is people-related, the more people they have, the better.
- By profitability or liquidity: do they have money to spend?
- By source of income: If they're publicly funded, can you provide something that aligns with the purpose of that spend?

Once you've decided some filtering criteria, you can filter your total available market into groups, and sideline (but don't forget) those that don't fit. You can then mix and match. If you know customers in your target market are in the UAE and have over 500 employees, then you can easily filter for these companies.The more criteria you identify, the better your targeting of customers and the more chance of closing a sale.

Ways to identify your target market 2: Referral partners

Referral partners are businesses that have the same target market as you, but are not competitors. You're allies. For instance, if you're selling microwave ovens, your referral partners might be businesses like kitchen fitters or microwave dish manufacturers.

Many companies have built their business around referral partners. They're invaluable sales tools and can help you identify businesses to pop into your target market.

Using referrals: Peter's story 1

We worked with a high-end relocation company that went the extra mile for their customers. They added value in so many ways: helping newcomers to find schools, places to live, helping with connecting utilities etc. But they were disappointed in their closing ratio as it was just 8%. They had no problem identifying potential prospects – normally HR departments of large companies who regularly relocated their staff – but these potentials weren't willing to pay the premium for the high-end service. We decided that these potentials were not, after all, our client's target market.

So we worked on finding non-competitive organisations who had the same target market as our client. Perhaps we could get referrals. One salesperson had a great idea – her friend worked in sales at a travel agency, so off to lunch they went for a discussion. It turned out that her friend gave her a list of companies that regularly booked through the travel agency and sent their staff business class or first class – a good indication that these companies were happy to spend extra money on their employees for travel, and might do the same for relocation.

At the end of lunch, our salesperson had not only built her target market by adding in "business travel agencies" as a type of business to her target market, but she'd identified 13 opportunities (actual named businesses). In the next 12 weeks her closing ratio rose from 8% to 23%.

Peter's story 2: Don't be shy about asking for referrals

I worked with a print salesperson who had a good success rate with referrals – over 60%. But he didn't add many to his opportunity pipeline each month, because he wasn't being proactive. Customers gave him referral names or asked other companies to contact him. He was a little shy and didn't want to be too aggressive with asking for referrals. He agreed to put a straw in place – at the end of every customer meeting, he'd ask "'Do you know anyone that would be interested in this type of printing?".

It worked. Despite only getting two extra referrals a month, he usually closed one of them. This might not sound much, but let's look at the data: he grew his customer base of 50 customers by 12 new clients each year, just by asking a simple question.

Ways to identify your target market 3: Existing and past customers

If you're not selling for a new business, it's useful to reflect on existing and past customers. What types of businesses are they? What sectors do they operate? What are the criteria or issues that **made** them buy from you?

Building your target market: some activities

- Complete a segmentation exercise (by industry, area etc).
- Review appropriate publications e.g. trade magazines.
- Attend networking events and build your contacts list.
- Solicit referrals whenever and wherever possible.
- Analyse existing clients: where do they trade? What other departments do they have?
- Conduct competitor research.

Some straws: Finding and managing opportunities

- Review your target market before you start contacting.
- Always ask for referrals at the end of a customer meeting.
- Review those referrals – are they the right ones?
- Build good relationships with the right referral partners.
- Keep track of the source of opportunities in your pipeline. You may spot a trend for types of businesses you can sell to, to develop your target market further.

CHAPTER 4:
All about opportunities

What's this about?

In this section you'll learn all about what opportunities are, how to get them and how to manage them. Opportunities are important because these are how you make your sales. No opportunity? No sale.

What's an opportunity?

An opportunity is an organisation that you think you have a good chance of selling to, either now or in the future.

An opportunity is not the same as a lead, so what's the difference?

- A lead is a piece of information that suggests sneakily in your ear, "There may be a chance to sell to this company. How exciting!" A lead isn't an opportunity. It's just the first sniff of a possible opportunity.

- An opportunity is a lead that you've **qualified** i.e. made a decision to pursue it, based on some parameters that you've pre-defined.

Here's an example:

Let's say you provide an online recruitment platform for HR teams. You've worked out you can only make a profit if you sell to a company with more than 200 employees, in the hospitality sector. You met an HR team leader at a conference and they're super-interested in what you do. You check out their company online and they've about 1200 employees worldwide, in the right sector. You think "Heck, yes, that qualifies." and, bang, that's an opportunity. If the company turned out to be three people and their dog, then you'd think "Nope, this business is too small to sell to." It's not an opportunity.

All about qualification

Qualification is the process of filtering the leads from your total available market so that you end up with the opportunities: companies or sectors that you're confident are likely to buy from you, and that you will therefore actively work on now or in the future. These are the opportunities for your pipeline.

Why is qualifying important?

Lots of time and effort goes into working on an opportunity, so making sure you're focusing on the ones with more chance of success is key. The lower your closing ratio, the less likely your business profit won't cover the cost of the sales team. But there's also motivation and enjoyment to consider – it's no fun chasing opportunities that are never going to work. A salesperson is far more motivated when working on realistic opportunities.

How to qualify

You'll need a system. When you've a systematic approach, you won't have to reinvent the wheel: you'll apply a set of predetermined rules to your lead/sales possibility to determine if they qualify for the pipeline. A tried, trusted and tested methodology for qualifying is, wait for it, the qualification scorecard.

The Qualification Scorecard

The qualification scorecard helps you make the decision to pop an opportunity into the pipeline (or not). It doesn't override which opportunities you choose to work on if there are factors that mean you still want to work on it. The scorecard is there to give some consistency about your qualifying decisions, against some pre-decided criteria.

Qualifying criteria might be related to the industry, the profitability of your target organisation, whether you have a contact there already, whether you sell to competitors already: anything that will help you decide if a win here is likely.

A scorecard can be simple or complex, depending on your business, market, and products.

Putting together a simple scorecard

A scorecard can simply be "If this opportunity scores 3 out of 5, then they're in the pipeline."

A simple scorecard:

- Is the opportunity from an industry that buys our product?
- Are they located in an area where we can sell our product?
- Does their website have information that fits the same characteristics as businesses we usually have success with?
- Do they have more than 100 employees?
- Are they selling products that match businesses we've been successful with?

If an opportunity matches 3 (or 4, or 5, your choice) then you will have it as qualified on your pipeline.

When do you qualify?

Although qualifying happens typically to put opportunities into the pipeline, you can qualify (or re-qualify) at later stages, as more information comes in.

At the beginning of the process, you can qualify through some background checks, before you ever meet a prospect. Sometimes you'll qualify after a first meeting, because you find out that it's unlikely they'll buy from you. Often, companies have two qualification stages in their sale process.

How to find out if you actually need a qualification mechanism

We think that every business should have a robust qualification process, but, if you're hesitating, try this exercise:

1. Write down your closing ratio (the number of sales you get out of your total number of sales attempts). Let's say it's 20%; for every 10 sales proposals 2 of the opportunities say yes.
2. Draw a rectangle and mark off 20% . Draw a line splitting the 80% using the following criteria:
   - What percentage of the opportunities did not win because you did something wrong during the process?
   - What percentage of the opportunities did not win because nobody could have won them?

When we've done this exercise with clients, we've found that very often the line is drawn around the halfway mark, so we have used 40% in the diagram below: half of the 80%.

Not Target Market	Need to Improve	Won Deals
40%	40%	20%
SELLING SKILLS		

Diagram 1

You'll get two things from this exercise, hopefully:

- It'll be clear to you how many opportunities you're wasting your time on, and how you can put your time more successfully towards better targets.
- You can assess why those opportunities were never going to buy from you, and these reasons may inform your scorecard criteria.

When you qualify, you eliminate lost causes and so your closing ratio and overall results will improve. It's not rocket science. It's just a straw.

Peter's story: Getting round the tick box

We worked with a large multinational. When we started to work with them, their closing ratio was 5% and they had a target of 7%, which had been established by management and was just one of many KPIs for the sales team to jump over. Having a target of 7% meant that the sales team worked on anything they could.

We found out that it was industry standard to quote to everybody approached, even those the sales team knew they were not going to win.

We quickly filtered those that were not the target audience and, once qualified, we ensured that we did not approach any others in this category – because, if we don't approach them, we don't have to quote. Clever, huh? At the same time, we developed a plan to provide a very simple 'tick the box' quote to those that the sales team had already approached but knew they wouldn't win. This means, the team had jumped the bureaucracy hurdle with minimum fuss and effort, and stopped the no-hope opportunities from ever entering the pipeline. With only qualified opportunities to focus on, the team spent all its time on good opportunities and the closing ratio went through the roof. New business in this category rose by over 30% .

The moral of this story is that when you focus your efforts on qualified opportunities, you sell more stuff.

Some straws: Qualifying leads

- Create a qualification scorecard and assess each lead against it. Add it to the pipeline only if it qualifies as an opportunity.
- Continually review your opportunities and remove any that you feel have become no-hopers.

Types of opportunity

We've found it helpful to categorise types of opportunity, because it informs how we manage them. We categorise them as:

- Existing customers.
- Identified opportunities.
    - Type 1
    - Type 2
    - Type 3
- Unidentified opportunities.
- Lapsed clients.

Existing customers

Your customer base could be full of opportunities for:

- Selling more of your product, or a different product, to them.
- Selling to different departments or branches.
- Selling to their contacts e.g. suppliers, customers or other relationships.

It's important that you define what an existing customer is, to decide if it's an opportunity. You might decide that an existing customer is:

- Anyone you regularly sell to.
- Anyone you've billed within the last six months or later.
- Anyone you've billed within the last year.

Note that regular, recurring orders from customers aren't opportunities. An opportunity is something you have to bid, quote, submit a proposal for, or otherwise make an effort to win.

Customer definition is important because managing a customer is very different to managing an opportunity.

Your existing customer base will feed your pipeline with opportunities.

Managing existing customer opportunities — some activities:

- Regular meetings.
- Business updates.
- Meeting new contacts.
- Feedback surveys.
- Asking for referrals.

Identified and unidentified opportunities

Identified opportunities are businesses that:

- You know about.
- You know have a need for your product or service.
- You're doing something with that information (preferably in your pipeline).

If the opportunity is in your pipeline and being managed (e.g. it has a follow-up date and action allocated), then it's an identified opportunity.

If it's a business card sitting in a cardholder on a salesperson's desk, then it's an unidentified opportunity.

Another thing to take into consideration is that if a business fits into your target market but isn't interested in your product or services **at the moment**, it's still an identified opportunity.

Identified opportunities include opportunities that you know about and you:

- Are actively selling to (Type 1).
- Are not actively selling to, but you're keeping them warm (Type 2).
- Have sold to, but the sale hasn't yet fulfilled its potential: you may need a bit extra time to deliver an expected revenue level. Or maybe they've bought from you but what you've sold to them isn't up and running yet (Type 3).

Identified Opportunity Type 1: Actively selling to

You're actively selling to these opportunities, and don't you think it's the most exciting part of sales? You could be in the process of either understanding more about a business and what they are looking for, meeting them for the first time, offering a proposal, or negotiating and closing the deal – you'll be anywhere along the sales process.

Managing Type 1 opportunities — some activities:

- Researching the business.
- Meeting decision makers.
- Presenting proposals.

- Building and maintaining momentum.
- Identifying and demonstrating value.

Identified Opportunity Type 2: Keeping them warm

You're not actively selling to these opportunities, but you are keeping them warm. There are loads of legitimate reasons why you're not actively selling. Some might be:

- Businesses that have said, "Not right now, come back another time."
- Businesses that have rejected you in the past, but you want to keep in touch.
- Businesses that have bought from your competitor.
- A business (perhaps an existing customer) that's told you a sister company might need your product, but not for a few months.
- Lapsed clients: businesses that have bought from you in the past, but not for ages (it's up to you to define what 'ages' means).
- Opportunities you've identified within your client base (such as a new project they're starting in a few months), but you're not ready to approach them.

Keeping these opportunities warm means keeping in touch and adding value where you can, but not being a pain.

Type 2 opportunities are **future opportunities**. All of these may not be active now, generating revenue today, but they could be a main source of business potential for the future.

We believe that managing future opportunities is the most underrated part of selling. Salespeople don't often have the long-game patience to manage them, as it takes attention, organisation and effort, but managing future opportunities differentiates average performers from the high flyers.

Managing Type 2 opportunities — some activities:

The goal with these opportunities is simply to keep you top of mind. Over the years this group will build significantly, so you can't always offer a huge amount of time toward them, but staying in touch is key and proactively planning for this makes sure it happens:

- Regular phone calls.
- Email updates.
- Invitations to your corporate events.
- Occasional visits.
- Have regular reminder dates to follow up.

Identified Opportunity Type 3

These are the businesses with which you've made a first deal. Getting the purchase order or agreement signed is often perceived as the sale being closed.

Whew! You can relax.

Nope.

There's still work to be done, because to get the best out of this opportunity you'll need to make sure that your company delivers on what was agreed, and that you live up to the promises you made during the sales process. A bad first sales experience can turn off a client, and you can lose the business forever.

If they have a good experience, they will more than likely come back, even if there is a long period in between. If they're happy, they'll become an advocate for you. They'll tell other people. If they've had a bad experience, they'll tell even more people.

Your best result for a Type 3 is getting recurring business. And, of course, when business starts recurring, you can move this Type 3 into your existing customer bag of opportunities.

Managing Type 3 opportunities: some activities:

- Completing set-up paperwork.
- Arranging any logistical requirements.
- Babysit while onboarding.
- Gaining feedback and learning from it.

Unidentified opportunities

These are the mystery opportunities – you don't know who they are, you don't know where they are, but you know they're out there somewhere. If you know your market size, you can work out what this number is both in terms of the number of target customers and the value of the opportunity. If you don't know the market size it will be pure guesswork and any goals that you set will be speculative, but it's still a worthwhile exercise.

Working out your target market size: example

Let's say your target market is any SME with over 50 employees in a radius of 50 miles of your HQ. Do your Google search and you'll find 250,000 business licences in that area. Google further and you know that only 5% have over 50 employees. So you now have a total available market of 12,500 potential prospects. It's not 100% accurate but does give you an indication.

When you've done some research, you'll have extracted from the unidentified opportunities details of some businesses that you might have a chance to sell to. Yay! You've found some new Type 1 identified opportunities!

CHAPTER 5:
Your opportunity pipeline

What's this about?

In this section you'll learn all about your opportunity pipeline. What it is, how to make one and what goes into it.

Opportunity pipelines are important because they're the basis of how you manage your sales process. Opportunity pipelines act as control towers, rather than lists. They're a way of making sure you have all your bases covered.

What's an opportunity pipeline?

An opportunity pipeline is a sales tool that helps you identify, prioritise and manage the opportunities you've identified where you might be able to sell something to someone. Almost all of a salespeople's activities should directly relate to actions prompted by the pipeline, such as:

- Managing follow ups, so nothing is forgotten.

- Deciding how to manage an opportunity, based on its position in the pipeline.
- Identifying which areas of the pipeline are empty and need topping up with opportunities.
- Deciding which opportunities are clogging up the pipeline because they've been there too long.
- Deciding if the opportunities being worked on are the right-sized ones.

Wait, isn't it a funnel, not a pipeline? No. A pipeline is a management tool. A funnel is a process.

Funnel: You put things at the top of the funnel and they slowly get filtered out through the funnel stages.

Pipeline: The things in your pipeline can recycle through it, sit in a pipeline section for a bit, travel up a to-do list and, yes, maybe get kicked out eventually.

A funnel is a linear process. A pipeline can be more circular, with feed pipes and exit pipes.

Why is your opportunity pipeline important?

It's your control tower that guides your actions every day. It's your primary mechanism that keeps you focussed on what makes a salesperson truly successful. Your opportunity pipeline makes you ask the right questions, such as:

- Can I be doing more?

- Who's next for a follow up?
- Do I have a strategy for these opportunities?
- Are some opportunities dragging on too long? What should I do about it?
- Do I have the right split for new opportunities and those I've been working on?
- Should I do more prospecting?
- Am I focusing on the right opportunities?

If you don't have a pipeline, you're flying blind, and will waste a lot of time and effort on the things that don't bring you success.

So, let's find out how to make one.

Setting up your pipeline

Whether you have some supercool Customer Relationship Management (CRM) software or prefer to fiddle around with a basic spreadsheet, the information you'll need to set up your pipeline is broadly the same. Basically, your pipeline:

- Captures information about your opportunities.
- Records previous actions and next actions.

If you're creating a sales pipeline that's going to be used by lots of people, you need to make sure that:

- Everyone has a common understanding of the terminology you use.

- The pipeline is easy to access and easy to use, otherwise who's going to bother?
- Results are visible: it must be easy to see the state of each section of your pipeline.

Data for your pipeline

Here are some examples to get you thinking about what is appropriate for you, but remember it's always up to you to decide what's actually useful to you. Just pick the data that helps you, rather than making things complex. It's always a good idea to keep things as simple as possible.

1. Opportunity business name and contact details

You'll need this so you know who you're targeting. We probably didn't need to say this.

2. Relationship to you

Is the opportunity an existing customer, a past customer or a total stranger? Here's where you differentiate between whether they're a new or existing opportunity. We've found that many salespeople fall into two camps: either they go after new business and neglect their existing customers, or they get too comfy with their existing customers and forget about new business.

Setting a target for both new and existing opportunities helps you keep a balance and helps to maximise market opportunity.

3. Opportunity life cycle period

The lifecycle of an opportunity starts when you start working on it – it's in an 'active' phase.

An opportunity is in an active phase when you're working hard to push it through the sales process – you're usually busy with things like:

- Understanding your potential client
- Discovering more about what they might need
- Working out how what you're selling solves their problems
- Putting together a solution for them, and presenting it to them
- Negotiating or closing the deal

The opportunity lifecycle period indicates how long the opportunity has sat in the pipeline and it's important to know this, for two reasons.

First, opportunities that haven't started their lifecycle get forgotten. Second, the length of each opportunity's lifecycle tells you how productive a pipeline is. Just because someone has more opportunities in their pipeline, it doesn't make them more productive. You need to factor in ageing (of the pipeline, not the salesperson).

Here's an example:

You're Salesperson A. You've 10 opportunities in your pipeline and it takes you 2 months to get them through your sales process (maybe to a sale, maybe not). That's an average of 5 opportunities you're proposing to per month.

Your friend is Salesperson B. She's only got 7 opportunities in her pipeline. Before you feel superior, let it be known that she clears her opportunities in 30 days. That's 7 opportunities she's proposing to per month.

The moral of the story is that more opportunities doesn't mean more sales. It could mean they're sitting there longer. The faster you turn your opportunities over, the more productive you'll be. And, depending on your closing ratio, the more sales you'll make.

4. Opportunity value

There's no point making a big effort for a small sale, so it's a good idea to have some kind of estimate of what every opportunity is worth. Of course, hopefully you'll have done your homework on worth during the qualifying process, but sometimes it's not always straightforward.

However, in the meantime put in your guesstimate, which is better than a "don't know" or a "0". You need to understand the value of opportunities in the pipeline to be able to know if you're on target. As you get more accurate data you can always update it when you get it.

Handy sidenote: We've found that different salespeople are more comfortable with different value opportunities. This is useful to know if you're developing a salesperson and when you're planning your sales team structure.

5. Pipeline stage

This shows you where you are in the sale and provides a clear high-level snapshot of the health of your pipeline. You'll be able to identify where to focus in order to achieve your targets.

6. Last visited / contacted

You want to know that 'something' is happening with every current opportunity and this will show you the latest. It may be OK for an opportunity to be in the pipeline for a longer period of time, as long as they're contacted regularly and the opportunity remains genuinely alive.

7. Last moved stage

This tells you when the opportunity last moved to a different place in the pipeline. This will show you opportunities that have become stuck. You might be stuck in the gathering information stage, and not yet submitted a proposal. Or you may have submitted a proposal but the customer is taking their time to respond. Or perhaps they've provided lots of buying signals but you've still not closed the deal.

This is especially useful when managing sales teams as it clearly highlights trends: where individual salespeople struggle to make progress. Once you've highlighted a problem, something can then be done to solve it.

8. Product

If you have more than one product or service, then the product mix should be reflected in your pipeline. You need to show what product is being sold — or the lead product if you're offering more than one — and the pipeline should show at a glance if you or your salespeople are selling across all your products.

Alternatively, you may have a new product launch or special focus on one particular product, and you may focus on this product a lot more for a particular time.

9. Opportunity source

Keep track of how you found out about the opportunity and the type of opportunity it is (e.g. a catering company that needs your products for events). This is key data that will help you build your target market further. If you're successful selling to this company, you could be successful selling to similar companies.

10. Next activity

This is, in many ways, the most important stage of the pipeline because it directs your next action with the opportunity: make phone calls, have a follow up meeting or send an email, but whatever the system, it only will work if the data is entered. In our experience, the performance of many sales teams skyrockets when every salesperson enters the next activity with an opportunity every time.

Feeding the pipeline

We'll look at what you should put into your pipeline, and the types of information you'll need to be able to manage them properly.

What goes into your pipeline?

- Identified opportunities Types 1, 2 and 3.
- Opportunities with your existing clients.

Regular orders from customers aren't opportunities. You'll remember that an opportunity is something you have to bid, quote, submit a proposal for or otherwise make an effort to win. And of course, you've qualified it.

Some straws: Using your pipeline

- Always add in your next activity into your pipeline.

- Make sure that the tool you're using to manage your pipeline (e.g. your CRM or your spreadsheet) is easy to use.
- Update the pipeline every day.
- Don't forget to measure how long an opportunity has been sitting in the pipeline.

Is it working? Measuring performance

You'll only know if your opportunity pipeline management is working if you've:

- Set targets and
- Measured performance against those targets.

Measuring performance shows you not just if your pipeline is working, but it'll show you which areas need improving to enable you to perform better ie. sell more stuff.

Remember, you can't manage revenue directly. But what you can do is manage your revenue-growing activities. Even if you're currently over target, measuring where you're doing well will help you do even more of the right things, and maximise revenue further. If you do more of the right activities, and do them better, then you can't help but get more positive results.

Measuring is also important because what gets measured gets done.

Measuring performance makes sure you have a healthy pipeline

Everyone loves a healthy pipeline. When you look at your pipeline, we want you to get a nice warm glow about how healthy it is. A healthy pipeline is a happy pipeline. Happy pipelines contain right-value opportunities that are progressing along the way merrily, with lots of sales popping out as a result. There are no clogs, no blockages and the pipeline tool itself is updated everyday because it's easy to do so and your sales people like it.

Yay for a healthy, happy pipeline!

Sometimes it's easy to mistake a fat pipeline for a healthy pipeline. In our experience, when we've worked with organisations, the sales team has assumed their pipeline is healthy because, "there's a lot in there", or "there are some big deals in the pipeline that we're working on".

But what does this mean in practice?

- Does this mean there is any chance of winning these deals?
- What happens if they do not win those deals?
- Are there many (or enough) other opportunities coming through to be worked on next to ensure targets are still met?
- What percentage of all the opportunities in the pipeline are actually viable?

Fewer, better targeted opportunities in your pipeline are better than a load of not-so-good ones.

It's not surprising that many sales teams can misread the usefulness of their pipelines, When you look at your pipeline, your gut might be telling you that it must be healthy because:

- There are a good number of opportunities there.
- The opportunities seem to be progressing.
- The opportunities seem to be of the right value.

But to find out for sure whether your pipeline is healthy or not, you need to start measuring.

KPIs: How to measure performance

Yes, it's time to bring the key performance indicator (KPI) out.

KPIs help you know where you are today, so you can focus on the right activities for maximum success.

KPIs are data, and without data, you don't know whether things are going well, or not. You need to know what's working and what's not, so that you can take action to improve performance. KPIs show you where the problems are, and where they aren't.

Another reason why managing KPIs is so important is that they help even top performing salespeople identify where they can improve. For example, if you're closing 50% of your opportunities and working on six opportunities a month, you'll be winning three. But if you made a teeny tiny bit more effort and worked on eight opportunities per month and retained your 50% closing ratio, you'd win four. Suddenly you'll have grown your business by 33%. Well done, you!

KPIs are good, but don't go overboard

We've found that companies can set salespeople so many KPIs that the salespeople become focused on meeting these and forget that their job is to sell. We've seen organisations with more than 30 separate sales KPIs, which is ridiculous and overwhelming for any salesperson. Your sales reports might look good but your revenue won't.

So, which activities should you measure?

The key is to identify the critical numbers that are relevant to your selling activity and focus on the ones that have the maximum impact. Selling is all about numbers, but all about the right numbers. It's also about a mixture of numbers: for instance, just focussing on call rates might improve your call rates and your results, but if you measure nothing else, you'll miss out on other opportunities to maximise quality and results.

We've found that it's best to focus on a few KPIs that measure the activities that have the biggest impact on success, and we have six favourites:

1. **Call rates:** how many visits with clear objectives are being made?
2. **Opportunities being worked on:** how many proposals have been made, and are these still live?
3. **Closing ratio:** how many targets say yes to a sale? How many say no?
4. **Time opportunity in pipeline:** how long does it take to work on a deal?
5. **Value per opportunity:** how much is the business worth?
6. **New/existing business ratio:** how many meetings are for new business, out of the total meetings?

Pipeline management in practice: when things are not what they seem

Measuring performance means that you can get the story of what's really going on with a pipeline. Here's an example:

Let's say your sales team is working on 30 active opportunities, against a target of 20 active opportunities. Looks good so far! There's "a lot in there". But if we measure a few things, we might see a completely different story. It might look like this:

- 25 of the opportunities have been in the pipeline for over 90 days, but the turnaround time of the opportunity for this industry is 30 days. This might indicate that the sales team are reviewing the same opportunities over and over again, and this means it's likely these opportunities will never be successful.
- Only three of the 30 opportunities are new business. It looks like the sales team are relying on existing

customers to give them additional business. This is good news but suggests that opportunities for new business are not being maximised.
- The average value of these opportunities is USD 1,500, but the target business profile is USD 5,000. Suddenly it doesn't look so good. Either the target customer size is incorrect, or the team is working on less valuable opportunities.
- Only 2 of the 30 opportunities focus on the right product for the business strategy. This means 28 of the opportunities are focussed on the wrong product, which will affect the success of the business strategy.
- The closing ratio is 15% but the target is 40%. Why are deals not closing? Are the team choosing the wrong opportunities to work on? Or is 40% too high for the industry? When there's a mismatch, it's worth looking at the accuracy or realism of the targets as well as the possible reasons for the results.

Every pipeline tells a story, if you look at the right things. It's important to measure more than one KPI, but not so many that your head falls off and the data becomes meaningless. If you start from a KPI that you want to improve – for example, number of opportunities that have the target business value – you can play with the rest of the KPIs to see if, by changing the numbers. For instance, you might do this by being more strict with qualifying parameters, to make sure only opportunities with the right business value enter the pipeline. You might assess if you're offering the right product to the right opportunity – perhaps the value of a deal might increase with a different product.

Some straws: Managing performance

- Identify no more than six areas of your pipeline to measure, and set realistic targets.
- Review your pipeline activities every week and plan your activities for next week, based on what you find.

CHAPTER 6:

Approaching potential customers

What's this about?

In this section you'll find out who you should be approaching to make a sale, and the best way to approach them.

The key to approaching potential customers correctly is to understand them, and then to pitch the correct proposal to the correct person. The correct person is the person who has the power to make the decision to buy from you. This person is called the **decision maker**, and they're not always the person you think it should be.

Who are decision makers and why are they important?

During a sale, if you're pitching to the person who has the authority to make the decision to buy, then you're far more likely to close the deal. There are simply fewer barriers to success. But there are other reasons, too:

- Selling to the right person has a huge impact on your closing ratio, and that's good for your figures.
- If you're selling to the wrong person, you're wasting a lot of time.
- Decision makers give you more information about the true potential of any deal.
- Decision makers are likely to commit more quickly and often the size of the contract will be bigger. Nice!

Who influences a sale?

It sounds simple, but it's not. If you're dealing with multiple contacts in an organisation, it's not always clear on how they'll affect your chance of selling. We've found that there are three categories of people who may be involved in a sale:

1. **Decision maker:** This is the person who is authorised to make the decision to buy what you're selling. They may or may not be the person who signs the contract – it's worth remembering that an authorised signatory may have little, if anything, to do with the buying process.
2. **Influencer:** These are the people who have an impact on any buying decision but don't make the final call on who to buy from. It's important to understand how strong an influencer they really are. Influencers might be secret decision makers. For example, if we think the decision maker is the person who signs off on the

deal, but they sign off on every deal their influencer colleague puts in front of them without question, then their influencer colleague is really the decision maker.
3. **User:** These are the people who are actually going to use, or be impacted by, what you're selling. We've rarely met a user that doesn't influence a sale in some way.

The Web of Influence

It would be lovely if clients put down a trail of cakes from the car park to the door of the real, true, actual decision maker, to make it easy for us salespeople to find them, but this hasn't happened yet. Instead, we need to understand the Web of Influence, which we put in capitals to make it sound like a thing. It is a thing. If you understand the concept of the Web of Influence, you won't break down crying when you are flailing around still looking for that decision maker.

The Web of Influence will help you. It's the understanding that decision makers, influencers, and users — and you — are all interconnected. This means that, whoever you're talking to in an organisation, you have the power to influence them. And, don't forget, they talk to each other when you've gone home. Here are some strands you might like to knit into your own Web of Influence, like some kind of weird sales spider:

- Having a good relationship with people in a procurement department can make life easier.
- Talking with users to find out pain points and be interested in their work. These are key people that have important information that can help you drive home the value of your proposal.

- Having other supporters helps you gather useful inside information.
- Always be nice to everyone. The security guard. The receptionist. The cleaner. (And why wouldn't you, anyway?)

Identifying the decision maker

Reason would tell you that you can identify the decision maker by their designation. Designation is usually the title after a person's name on their business card.

In this case, reason is a bit of an idiot. A person's designation alone will not always give you the full picture. It'll give you some useful information but there's still plenty of work to do.

For example, once we had two different meetings with two different people working for the same client, who were both designated as logistics managers.

When we got to the customer's premises, one of the logistics managers was sweeping out the warehouse, as keeping the warehouse clean was part of his job description. The other had over 400 staff and told us all about his Mercedes Benz company vehicle (and, unconsciously, his lack of self esteem). Both had the same designation, but different responsibilities. Both could be decision makers, or neither of them. We couldn't assume that the logistics manager with the fancy car had the authority to buy loads of stuff. Maybe the logistics manager sweeping the warehouse had the authority to actually buy a warehouse.

Designation alone does not help us when considering the decision maker in a target organisation.

Sometimes the industry you sell in to can hide the decision maker from you. For instance, in the construction industry, a contractor might be your client, but they might not be the decision maker, or even have much influence. Their client's client might be the real decision maker. Even a consultant may be the decision maker.

The point of this? Never assume.

What about procurement?

OK, if someone's designation has something to do with procurement – buying stuff – then it should be checked out. We need to understand where procurement fits into the decision making process in the organisation. If you've been selling for a long time, you'll have heard the "Oh, I can't decide that, procurement makes all the decisions" thing quite a lot. But in our experience, in most cases they don't. People in procurement don't decide on every investment that a company makes.

Procurement's role is to source, often at the lowest price. They may play the game that they want the best value, but their performance is not based on how much they spend, but on how much they save. They don't often have the final say. They have strong input into the buying decision, but any professional company will have an evaluation process that requires sourcing the best products and services that can provide the best value to their business.

As sales people, we're selling value. And the perceived value will come from who will be directly impacted by your product or service — the user.

The reality is that, in most instances, what is best for the business will always come first. If you can find and demonstrate value to the person or department that understands, then you have most likely identified the true decision maker.

Sometimes you might have to deal with internal dynamics and wrangling: the user's goals are different from procurement's goals, and that means you'll need to be on top form making your product so compelling and valuable to the user. Give them the ammunition they need to make a business case.

What you need to find out

The key to identifying the decision maker lies in understanding your customers. If you want to be able to understand what's going on within your target organisation and to be able to pitch the correct proposal to the correct people, here's what to find out::

- What are the roles each designation is playing? This will be different from business to business, so it's important to know how influential a certain position may be. You can benchmark against other known customers, but don't assume that what has worked with one will be the same in another.
- What are the relationships like within the business? Who listens to who? Who has confidence in a certain

person and who doesn't? You may need to get different people on your side to overcome other people who may not be on your side. It's not quite Game of Thrones, though.

- Who will benefit from what you're selling? These people will have the most buy in.
- Who might be disadvantaged by what you're selling? How can you reduce the negative impact on them?
- How strong is procurement? They will always play a role, which is normally price related, but can usually be overcome through skilled negotiation. It would be good to understand early on how influential they may be and act accordingly.

Why don't salespeople try to meet the decision maker more often?

We've found that many salespeople don't make a big effort to identify and get access to the decision maker. Here's why:

- They don't want to upset their existing contact.
- They're comfortable dealing with the existing contact.
- It's hard work. Much harder than meeting with somebody who is willing to meet with you.
- They're on autopilot, ticking the boxes for "number of meetings with contacts" without focusing on whether they are still meeting with the right contact or the impact it has on their success rates.

Some straws: Approaching potential customers

- Spend time gaining enough understanding to work out to whom you should be selling.
- But don't forget to qualify. Sniffing out the decision maker can take time and effort, so don't forget to qualify a potential client to make sure your effort is worth it. In your initial investigation, you might find that:
  - You can't find any value for the customer — which means you can't actually demonstrate it.
  - The sale might not be big enough to warrant a massive effort.
  - You're too busy with fully qualified opportunities to be able to find out all of this.

CHAPTER 7:
Getting the meeting

What's this about?

In this section you'll learn some tips and tricks on how to actually get a first meeting with a potential customer.

Once you've found a promising contact in your target organisation, it's time to try to get a meeting with them.

It can be very daunting making the first, cold-ish move on a possible client. But remember that rejection is just part of the job. Don't take it personally. But if you can reduce your rejection rate by increasing the number of times you can get meetings with decision makers, you'll have a massive impact on your sales.

Don't take our word for it. Look at the numbers. Let's take an example:

A deal is worth 10K USD. Your closing ratio when you secure a meeting with a decision maker is 50%

For every 20 attempts at securing a meeting, you get four meetings with the decision makers. Apply your closing ratio and you have two wins: 20K in the bank. Yay! Who cares you were rejected 16 times? Not you.

But, if you improve how you go about getting those meetings, and now you get in front of a decision maker six times out of 20, you sell to three (that 50% closing ratio) and make 30K. That's a 50% increase in sales. How amazing do you look now, even though you've still been rejected 14 times? Really amazing.

More meetings with decision makers = more wins. It's just science. Probably.

Should your first meeting always have to be with the decision maker? Ideally, but not necessarily. The original meeting (i.e. your first ever meeting) with a possible client might be with a user, a department head, someone in procurement, none of whom might be the decision maker. But we still need that original meeting because we'll never get access to decision makers or make a sale if we don't get the original meeting.

Making appointments

This is the starting point of your sales process and you'll be focussed on turning initial interactions into meetings. It has a significant impact on your revenue results. You can reach out to your potential client in different ways: could be by email, could be by calling them, could be through a basket of cookies. It's not usually done through interpretive dance, but you do you.

It's important to measure what percentage of calls that turn into meetings. Then, if you make one extra call or send one extra email, you can measure how one tiny straw impacts your results.

How to do it:

There are different ways to interact for the first time with a potential client. Here's what we've found to be super-effective:

Use introductions and references

Introductions and references are powerful. They are one of the most successful ways of getting that first meeting. In our experience, this has the highest rate of success.

If you're introduced or recommended by somebody your target contact knows, and hopefully respects and likes, you've hurdled over the social proof barrier and reduced the number of completely unsolicited calls that you need to make. "Ah," thinks your potential contact, "Dave rates this person. I already trust them a bit. I am not totally weirded out by them calling me."

How to ask for introductions

Yep, this can feel awkward sometimes but we need to bite the nettle and practise.

1. Dig the well before you get thirsty

To help get comfortable with asking for introductions, it's important to dig the well before you get thirsty. This works both literally and metaphorically and supports one of our favourite rules – the rule of reciprocity. Do stuff for other people, just for the fun of helping other people, and you'll find that you'll be helped in return at some point.

Now, be careful. Do it cynically and they'll sniff out manipulation. Spend time developing your network, warming up contacts, digging the well by being helpful and useful to your connections.

2. Choose your connection

Because you've researched your potential client, you'll be looking for connections (not people) between the people you know and your target's industry or background.

3. Ask nicely

It's important that when you ask a connection for an introduction, they've got to want to do it. You're a salesperson, so your job is to persuade.

If you've already prepared the ground by being a decent, useful person, not at all out to get an introduction, a simple request might be enough:

"Hi Dave, would you mind putting me in touch with your connection Ravi at Krazy Kookies plc? They're expanding into ice-cream and I'd like to find out if he'd be interested in some new flavors we're developing. Would that be ok?"

If you call your connection with a "Hey, Dave, haven't seen you for 30 years, can you introduce me to your multi-billionaire father-in-law CEO of MaxCorp? Awesome! See ya!" it probably won't work, and you can see why.

But if you call your connection showing how you want to help their contact be successful in their role, it'll increase the chances of your connection agreeing to make the introduction:

"Hi Dave, would you mind putting me in touch with Ravi at Krazy Kookies plc? I know that he's newly responsible for sustainability, and I think I can help him reduce his manufacturing plant's emissions by 50%."

4. Keep up the momentum

When your connection has committed to the introduction, it's time to politely go to the next stage of your request. If you're in front of them, grab your courage and ask them if they can contact them now, so you can arrange an appointment time while you are there.

Often salespeople settle for an email address, a phone number on a piece of paper, or an introductory email, which are fine as at least you're further forward, but the less personal touch leaves more work to be done to get that meeting.

Making the first call

The objective of your first call isn't to make a sale. It's to get an appointment. That's it... nothing more.

This is where you use the magic of your elevator statement. Yes, these still exist and they do so because they're effective.

In the old days, the elevator statement (or you may have heard it as 'elevator pitch') was a short, succinct, persuasive and ready-to-go message that, in the unlikely event you were ever stuck in an elevator with a decision maker for a short time, you'd use to get their interest.

However, we like to reframe the elevator statement as a short message you use to quickly elevate your brand or what you're selling.

Elevator statements are useful in all parts of the sales process, including right at the start, when you're ready to get in touch with your contact for the first time. But it's important to remember about balance. Professional selling is about understanding the customer, and this means asking questions rather than making statements. However, if your contact asks about you, your elevator statement can be very effective in making them feel confident that you're credible, and that it's worthwhile for them to answer your questions.

You won't have long to make an impact when making an initial contact. You'll have about 20 seconds. 20 seconds is the amount of time that an average person will pay attention to an incoming statement, so, whether by phone or on email, ensure your elevator statement is ready. You are trying to convince your contact (hopefully the decision maker) to meet with you, so your statement should differentiate you from the competitors, and make it clear that what you're selling can positively impact their business. You'll need to illustrate some value for them to want to meet you, but don't overcomplicate things as at this stage — you're not looking to fix all their issues. You're just looking to fix the meeting.

Even if you do get more than 20 seconds on a call, you'll still need to prepare and be creative along the way because, although you're prepared for your call, your target won't be. They're probably in the middle of something else and they may not really be listening. You need to be sharp.

If you've prepared well, and you're speaking to the person you want to meet with, your only goal is getting them to say yes to a meeting.

So, how do you do that? Especially if you've just got 20 seconds (if you're lucky) and your contact is probably in the middle of something much more fun or important for them than a cold sales call.

It's important to remember that:

- Customers do not want to feel as though they are being sold to. Who does?
- Customers want to feel served and supported.

Here's a four-step approach to using that 20-second opportunity effectively. In our experience, it gets the best results i.e. more meetings.

1. Introduce yourself (three seconds)

Be polite, state your name and keep smiling. Your customer will hear your smile in your voice.

2. Build credibility (four seconds)

Introduce your company in a way that will elevate your company. Use its strengths, its market share, the value it brings to customers, or anything else that's impressive — and relevant to your contact.

E.g. "I'm calling from Dubai Office Products, and we hold one of the largest stationary stocks in the Middle East."

E.g. "I'm Peter calling from MaxSale Solutions, the only company in the Middle East that focuses on improving the activity and effectiveness of your salespeople".

3. Create interest (eight seconds)

This is where you'll drop in why your contact would want to meet with you. What's in it for them? During your preparation you'll have identified issues that you can support, or interests that your contact company might have. Things like:

- The competition. If you are calling a pharmaceutical company and you're dealing with another well-known brand in the market, then your way of creating interest may be: "We've recently completed a project with Dubai Pharmaceuticals, and they have publicly stated that our program was responsible for their recent outstanding performance."
- Your current customers, if they're well known: "We've recently worked with Big Company where we improved their revenue performance by 45% through two simple improvements to their sales team's skills."

4. Making the appointment (five seconds)

This will take practice, and you'll need to build your confidence on this one. At this stage, your potential customer has remained silent, and after the first 16 seconds we hope their phone is still firmly pushed up against their ear. Now it's time to make it easy for them to say yes to a meeting.

The best way is to make sure the reason is about them and not about you. If you start mentioning your products, then your customer will feel sold to and feel pressured into buying from you. So avoid things like:

- I'd like to come in and see how we can work together.
- Which of our products or services can help you?
- I'd like to come in to present our company profile to you.

- I'd like to introduce my company to you.

Why the heck should your potential customer care what you'd like to do?

It's better to focus on them – on supporting or serving them. Anything around industry or technical updates can be very effective. Make sure it requires as little commitment as possible from them.

- I'd like to tell you more about the latest industry initiatives. Would you be free to meet at 10 tomorrow morning so I can provide an update?
- I'd like to tell you more about the latest industry initiatives. Is it better for me to come past at 10 am tomorrow or two in the afternoon?

Nice and easy, very direct.

Then what happens?

Once you've asked for the meeting, one of three things can happen:

1. You get the appointment. Go, you! Resist the urge to shout "Whoop!" and jump around the room. Say thanks, goodbye and hang up. You can find out where they are and any other details through their reception, if they haven't let you know. It's important not to reconfirm as if you call back you are giving them a chance to back out.

2. They say they're not interested, and it's their right to. But it's also OK to ask them why they're not interested (in a polite way). This may open a conversation and, at the very least, give you more information about the contact, the company or its culture. Every time you answer a question or make a statement, return to trying to close for an appointment.
3. They'll ask you questions. Great! More opportunities to support and serve. Again, every time you answer a question, return to trying to close for an appointment.

Some straws: Getting the meeting

- Develop your own elevator statement but make sure that it's flexible so that you can fit the interests of your target. Do this in the Create Interest section.
- Make sure there's a clear and useful reason for them to meet you, and that there's very low commitment from their side.
- Challenge yourself with every customer, new or old, and question whether you're meeting the right contacts. If not, take action.

CHAPTER 8:

Your first meeting

What's this about?

In this section you'll learn how to prepare for that vital first meeting with a potential customer, and how to create a good impression. You'll also find out how to create rapport, and how to ask the right questions that will get you the all-important information about your potential customer's needs.

Why preparing properly for your first meeting is important

This is a slight no-brainer, but preparing properly for your first meeting with your client:

- Makes you look, sound and be professional.
- Gives you an objective, which will give you confidence and direction.
- Helps you uncover information and opportunities.

- Will show your prospect that you've been trying to understand them and their business. You've made an effort. Well done you!
- Makes it a whole lot easier for you to gain the next step.

Don't treat your first meeting as generic. It's never good to wing it. Preparing thoroughly is good, but 'thoroughly' doesn't mean days of prep. If you over-prepare, you may end up making assumptions about what your client wants or needs. The trick is to find a balance: know a little about the client, be ready with questions that are aimed at uncovering needs, and make sure you know your product or service inside out.

How to prepare for your first meeting:

1. Decide your objective or objectives for the meeting. You'll need a clear idea of what you want to achieve. This will depend on the context of the first meeting. A common objective is to find out their situation, their business needs, and opportunities for what you're offering to address this. It could be about identifying where you can add value. It may be more about understanding the decision-making process, identifying other stakeholders within your client's business, or looking for a referral. Having an objective gives you direction, but whatever objective you have, you're usually looking to discover something about your prospect that will help you sell to them. The first meeting is often called 'the discovery meeting." Well, we call it that, anyway.

2. Don't make assumptions about what they might need. Be open to what they might say.
3. Do a little research about your client. Check them out personally on LinkedIn, to put them in context. Find out if you have connections in common and get a little info about their work history to help you understand their experience, or look for commonalities to build rapport. Don't do so much that they think it's a bit weird.
4. Check out the company operations and history. Look at the company website to get a feel for what they do, and how they like to be perceived. Find out where their product comes from and who they sell to. Looking at their past projects or customers can be very useful: if there's no case studies or press releases on their website, a quick Google search will help.
5. Prepare some questions that you hope might uncover their business needs. You might not need them, because when you're in the meeting, it's important that you're led by the client, but questions are a good way to kick-off fact-finding.

Peter's story: When it goes wrong

I accompanied a salesperson to a first meeting with a potential client. On the way to the meeting, he told me that he knew exactly what this customer was looking for. He had worked with their competitor and saved them thousands of dollars with his solution for their manufacturing plant. He was super confident that, because it had worked in the past, it would work now.

At the meeting, the salesperson asked a few perfunctory questions. I could tell he wasn't interested in the answers. He then dominated the meeting explaining how he could improve their manufacturing line. Being told how he should run the plant really upset the potential client, who, through gritted teeth, asked for the details by email and sent us on our way. Outside, the salesperson told me how defensive the customer was, and how he didn't listen,

Did he get the sale? No. All he showed the client was how arrogant and assumptive he was.

But this story does have a happy ending. A couple of years later a sale was made. Same solution but different salesperson with a different approach. They sought to understand the client first, and then gently linked their solution to the client's problem, without telling him how to run his business. It's common sense and common decency, really.

The moral of this story is that making assumptions and knowing what's good for your prospect is not part of preparing for your first meeting.

Some straws

- Set yourself clear objectives of what you want to achieve.
- Find out who your client is, what the company does, some of its projects and have a think through how your product might help: but never assume.

- Don't over prepare, as this may lead to assumptions that could prevent you from truly understanding your client's situation and needs.

Creating a good first impression

Here's where you find out why first impressions matter, and how to make a good one.

What's a first impression? (because asking questions is good)

Our definition of a first impression is: What you make people think/feel/believe about you when they meet you for the first time.

Here's what we know about first impressions:

1. It only takes seven seconds for someone to create their first impression of you.
2. It's super difficult to get rid of a first impression.
3. The first impression of you is the most lasting.

and, the kick in the teeth:

4. You'll never, ever, ever get a second chance to create a good first impression. Ever.

Why are first impressions important?

They're important because they affect how people feel about you, and, as a result, how they react to you.

In a sales situation, first impressions can be the difference between making an all-you-can-eat sale with a now-customer-for-life, or being thrown by your Marks & Spencer's tie out of the window. From the fourth floor.

Here's a less fatal example: say you're meeting with a potential customer for the first time. Now, they obviously don't hate you, but there's something about their first impression of you that makes them feel unsure of you. This means they won't open up when you try to understand their needs. And this means you won't get the information you need to make exactly the right solution or offer for them, in the way they need it. Will you make the deal? Probably not.

The slippery thing about the first impressions we make is that we're not aware of them. We don't pay attention. Sure, we'll pay attention to the first impressions we get from other people, but it's much harder to look at ourselves.

What sucks about good first impressions

Making a good first impression is important, but it doesn't make your potential customer think, "Wow, I want to do business with this person forever". Creating a good impression is just you being a normal, decent human being. They won't notice a good impression, but they'll sure notice a bad one.

It's a bit like finding a slug on your otherwise-normal Friday night pizza.

Good impression = Not a bad impression. It's just science.

How to make a good first impression i.e. a not-a-bad-first impression

A lot about making a good impression is common courtesy.

Be on time

We'll say it. Being late is rude. It suggests you don't value other people's time. Being late is No 1 on the Hot 100 of crappy things sales people do.

Your potential client won't sit you down at the end of your meeting and give you some useful feedback about how you being late made them feel. But this doesn't mean they didn't feel it. But they'd be thinking that:

- You don't value their time or their business.
- You don't respect them.
- You're unprofessional.
- You represent your company, so your company must be a bit rubbish.

A lot of sales is putting the customer first. Imagine them twiddling their fingers waiting for you, unable to properly get on with their work, looking at their watch as the minutes tick by. That's not putting them first. And excuses don't cut it. Bad traffic? Parking problem? Welcome to the normal world. Of course there's traffic, of course parking is a nightmare, but we all know this.

How to be on time

- Do your prep: Know where you're going, how long it takes to get there, where to park, and where to park if the first parking place is on fire.
- Give yourself much more time than you think you need. Build time into your schedules and arrive early.
- If you know that you're going to be late, call ahead in good time. Calling five minutes before the meeting starts is not good. It will make you seem disorganised.

The joy of arriving early

Getting to your client 20 minutes early means a stress-free, relaxed you, and time to:

- Be polite and lovely to the security guy or gal, the receptionist and whoever else. Good first impressions with your client's people are free!
- Powder your nose, or elsewhere, and make sure you look your best.
- Make your own impressions of your client's organisation.
- Bust open your laptop out and catch up on work, or review your sales strategy.

Be presentable

Being presentable doesn't mean that you have to wear the full business suit every time. It means wearing the clothes that are appropriate for the meeting, and what your client would expect you to wear.

It's a good idea to mirror your client as much as possible. Got a meeting with a traditional bank? Smart business wear in your gender's flavor is appropriate. If you're meeting a surf shop owner, you'll probably be fine going for a more casual look, but bikini and flip-flops may be going too far. If in doubt, plan to be as smart or a little smarter than your client, to make sure that you're showing respect. "Fitting in" with your client will also make you feel more confident.

If you're not a natural suit person, and feel that you're not being true to yourself by wearing businesswear, think of it as your camouflage. You're putting on the clothes that tell the client, "I'm just like you." If you want to maintain your identity, you can always wear your PVC pants underneath. No one except you will know.

Staying presentable

Some days you might be rushing around to five different meetings. Make sure you give yourself time for a quick check in the mirror before you go into the client, to give yourself the thumbs up and get the spinach off your teeth.

Be polite

This is really a no-brainer. Being polite is just human decency and the very least your client can expect from you. If you're sitting down when they arrive, stand up. Wait until they invite you to move toward a certain area. Don't push through the door first. All remarkably simple good manners. There's nothing complicated here, but it's worrying how often we see salespeople forget this.

Be confident

If you've had to work really hard to set up the meeting, you might feel desperately grateful to your potential client. Being appreciative is important but you don't need to get down on your knees and worship them, metaphorically. Or even literally. When you go into any meeting be confident in yourself and your product. Your body language will project this, and make a strong first impression. Confident body language looks a bit like this:

- Clear eye contact as you head toward your client.
- Walk tall as you move.
- Use a firm handshake, if a handshake is appropriate. Firm means firm but you're not trying to break your client's fingers. This just demonstrates you're probably acting out some toxic masculine powerplay that was cringey even back in the 1970s. Make sure you're not giving the wet haddock handshake, either. Give the kind of handshake you'd like to receive.

Set your own standards

It's not often you'll receive feedback from your potential customer, especially when they never become a customer. If they thought you were rude, inappropriately dressed, looking a bit shoddy or treated their receptionist with arrogance, they won't tell you, and why should they?

Because you'll never be told why your first impressions fell flat, you need to set the bar for your own behaviour, and stick to it. What will be your own standards of behaviour?

Elevator statement or no elevator statement?

If your prospective client has already agreed to meet up with you, they probably know what you're about. But that doesn't mean you won't need some kind of introduction: if you're working for a well-known brand then you shouldn't need to do a full dive. But a brief overview will get the client more relaxed because it'll reassure them they're with someone, presumably credible, from a credible company.

Make sure that your overview is short and to the point: practice, time yourself and if your blurb is more than a minute, it's a fail. You don't want to send your prospect to sleep with a meandering origin story. If your prospect wants to know more, they'll ask. Remember that the goal of your face-to-face elevator oration is to make them feel comfortable, not to convince them to buy.

Some straws: Making a good impression

- Think back to your last five "first impressions:" meetings. Were you on time, presentable, polite, and confident? What could you do better or differently?
- Think of one area that you know needs improvement, but don't feel embarrassed, because we all have our blind spots and you are doing something about yours. Look with curiosity and kindness at yourself. For instance, if you know that you have a tendency to run late, think about how you could improve your punctuality. It could be as simple as estimating a set-off time, then making it 30 minutes earlier. It could be preparing your meeting clothes the night before.
- Create some rules of first impression behaviour for yourself.

Building rapport

In this section we'll show you ways to build rapport with your client.

What's rapport?

There are lots of different definitions of rapport, but you know when you feel rapport with someone. At its core, rapport is a positive relationship between people or groups. There's often a feeling of mutual trust, of harmony, and of being on the same side.

Why rapport is important

In sales, a good rapport has a great impact. If there's nothing to choose between you and another salesperson, but you have a better rapport with your client, the client will most always choose you. When your client trusts you and is comfortable with you, almost every part of the sale runs more smoothly and usually more quickly.

When to start building rapport

Rapport building starts before you've even met the client, when you first make the appointment, but your big opportunity for building big rapport is during your first meeting.

Build rapport by being human

The one thing that you and your client usually have in common is that you're both human. Talking with your client to find out or highlight other things you have in common can help to make the client think: "Oh, they're just like me." The key initially is to get them to open up.

In the bad old days we were taught to look for something in the client's office and use it as a topic to talk about. We found this only worked if we were genuinely interested in the "thing", otherwise it sounded like we were going through the ABC of selling.

The holy trinity of opening conversations is:

- Be interested in your client as a person, not a client.
- Ask interesting questions.
- Be authentic.

There are no hard and fast rules about what to talk about, but if you're naturally interested in people, you'll probably find this straightforward.

Peter's story: Having kids helps

"I've always enjoyed meeting clients for the first time, but, since I had children, I've found it much easier to build rapport with clients because they have kids, too. So, when I see pictures of kids, it's easy, and very human, to ask about them. Clients usually love talking about their children and that's a great start. It helps that I'm genuinely interested, too. The trials and triumphs of parenthood are certainly a great rapport builder."

We don't recommend that budding sales people have children just to build rapport with clients. That's going too far.

When it goes wrong

If the client catches even one whiff of inauthenticity, it's a bad start. Be authentic. Don't pretend that you're a Chelsea fan just because they're wearing the t-shirt. First, you could get caught out and they'll know you're a bit of a fraud. Second, that sweet rapport you wanted? Gone. And very difficult to build up again, unless you're willing to be honest: "You got me, I've no idea who plays left whatever for Chelsea. I just wanted you to like me."

Peter's story: How not to build rapport

The salesperson saw an American football on the client's desk and said, 'Wow, you like American football. I love it. It's great, isn't it?'. Then the client of course asked what team he supported. After an awkward silence the salesperson blurted, "The Boston Red Sox!". The client looked a little like he wanted to shove the football down the poor salesperson's throat but gently explained that the Boston Red Sox was baseball. The meeting after that did not go well.

Building rapport: some straws

- Do a little research on your client beforehand e.g. using their LinkedIn profile. If you find anything you think interesting (their degree, a hobby, volunteering), ask about it. There's nothing wrong with saying, "I stalked you a bit on LinkedIn and I noticed that you volunteer for the Cinnamon Trust. Are you walking a dog at the moment?"
- Observe your surroundings carefully before you get down to business. If you notice something you find personally interesting, it's possible that they're interested in it, too.

Gaining understanding

In this section, we'll show you how to gain a real understanding of your client's business and their needs. When you ask the right questions at the right time and, just as importantly, listen, you'll build information about your client and their potential needs. You could also call it fact finding, information gathering, learning or probing – there are many words for one thing – understanding.

Why is this important?

When you really understand your client and their needs, you'll have the information you need to be able to frame what you're selling in a way that aligns with, and adds value to, what they need.

Remember, this part of the process is about them, not you. Often, sales people are so wrapped up in their own experience and knowledge – their products, service, targets – that to clear their mind of all that and focus on the client can be pretty difficult.

Chatting to your client about your products without understanding what they need is like throwing your products at a wall and hoping one sticks. You're providing a solution. You're answering their prayers. So you better make sure you know what they're praying for.

In the majority of sales where there's no real choice between suppliers, the one who can show the impact of their product on the client usually gets the deal. And it's all done through gaining understanding.

Listening

Questioning is the main methodology for finding out what your client needs, as a basis for how you frame what you're offering, but it's just as important to listen.

Listening shows respect, but it also gives you solid clues about what the client is really telling you. It informs your next question, but is also just as informative as questioning. If you don't listen, you won't understand enough about their business to sell the value that your offer should bring. The client will know when you're not listening, too. If you're spilling out a list of questions by rote without interest in the answers, that's your rapport gone.

People stop listening because they're analysing the information they've just received, or are thinking of their next question. Poor listening is extremely common and something that's fairly easy to fix: write it down. Writing things down during a conversation works perfectly. If you hear something useful, jot it down to jog your memory, and then carry on listening.

If you're worrying that you won't remember your next question, don't. Your brain is faster than you think and, worse case scenario, you can ask the client for a few seconds to digest the information they've provided.

Asking questions

Asking questions is the foundation of finding where you can add value. If you don't ask questions, you won't understand the client. If you don't understand the client, you can't offer value, sell solutions or negotiate on anything other than price. Asking the right questions – and listening to the answers – are critical to any sale.

Your questions should relate to the response you've just received, and it could be something simple as probing further the information you've just been given. You'll have a plan of where you want the meeting to go, but there does need to be a sense of two-way conversation.

In theory, questioning is simple three-step process that feeds back into itself:

1. You ask a question.
2. The client answers, and you listen 100% to that answer.
3. You ask your next question.

Sounds simple. But, remember, your questioning should be about their needs, not your product.

About open questions

When you want the client to open up, it's time to use open questions. These are questions that stop your prospect using a simple yes or no answer. They encourage the prospect to think, expand and give more information that'll give you more clues as to how what you sell can help them.

Open questions often start with who, what, where, why, when, how:

- Why is that?
- How has this affected your relationship with your suppliers?
- What does that mean?
- When would you use this?

Closed questions don't give you rich information:

"Does that mean less sales?" "Yes"...

With closed questions, you don't always get the correct answer, because people are nice and it's easier to agree with you:

'Would that mean this will work better for you?' "Oh yes, of course."

Closed questions are good for clarity, if you've not quite understood something:

"So, do you sell cornish pasties in Moldova?" "No." End of.

About needs and requirements

In sales, needs and requirements are not the same thing.

A requirement serves a need. For example, you need to charge yourself up every morning so you require a damn good breakfast.

In a real-life situation, a client was losing business because they were losing calls. They were losing calls because their call system had no hunt group functionality: the ability to switch to a call centre agent if the first one is busy.

The need: to stop losing business

The requirement: a phone system with a hunt group functionality.

Salespeople need to respond to customers' needs.

The five (or however many you want) whys

To get to the need, keep asking why. Obviously, not in an annoying five-year-old child way. Get from requirements to needs in five (or so) whys. You can practise on yourself. If we gave you USD3,000 to spend (we won't), what would you spend it on?

Keep asking why, and you'll get to a need from a requirement. Here's an example:

Us: Hey, Salesperson X, here's USD 3,000 to spend. What are you gonna buy?

Salesperson X: A nice new business suit.

Us: Why?

Salesperson X: To look smart, stupid.

Us: Why do you want to look smart?

Salesperson X: It will create a good impression with customers.

Us: Why is this important?

Salesperson X: More chances to close sales.

Us: Why is this important?

Salesperson X: Success and more money.

So, if you're a suit seller, you'd be focussing on what your customer wants out of the suit (the need) rather than the fancy buttons and other features.

There may be lots of needs

There's not always one need to discover. More needs equals more opportunities. Your initial questions should scope out what other opportunities there may be.

Focus on them

Salespeople are often so into their own products that they forget their prospects' point of view. They narrow the focus on the colours they can provide, the speed of shipment or a single feature of what they're offering. When you're questioning, focus more broadly.

Instead of:

What are the colours you would like in the office?

ask

What environment are you trying to establish, and what would you like this environment to achieve?

Instead of:

How fast do you need to get the shipment there?

Ask

What's important for you when transporting your product from one location to the next?

Questioning techniques

We've found two simple techniques that cover most ground with any client, and that's because they're common sense and client-focussed. And, because we love an acronym, these two techniques are the:

1. U.S.E. method: use this for clients who want to buy something, but they're not using a competitor.

2. F.O.R method: use this for clients who are already buying from a competitor.

The U.S.E method

This is a technique to use when you are trying to sell to a potential client something that they have not bought or used before. It focuses on how you can add value to them or their business.

U is for **Understand** the clients requirements and needs. Why are they thinking about this purchase? What will it mean to them once they make this purchase? What is important to them when making the purchase? The key here is to clear your mind of what you are selling, and be focused on your client's requirements and the reasons behind the requirements. Understanding questions are general: mostly you're listening and keeping your focus on identifying areas you can help your client.

S is for **Specify**. Specify questions happen when you've identified an area during the Understanding phase that you want to probe further. Specify questions drill down into the details and might sound like, "Can you tell me a little more about that part of your operation? Why do you think this is happening? Can you just take me through the steps in that process?"

E is for **Enlarge**. Once you've identified an area where you feel that you can add value, dig deeper. Enlarge questions are looking for the consequences of the issue and might sound like, "What would happen if you did not get packaging on time? How does this type of occurrence affect your customer satisfaction?"

The F.O.R method

Use this questioning technique for clients that you've already sold to.

F stands for **Fact Finding.** This step is for you to understand their business, goals and challenges. Possible questions could be 'What are your goals for this year?', 'Which products and services would help you become successful?', 'What areas of your business need more focus?'

O stands for **Obstacle**. By now you'll have a good understanding of their business and here's where you're identifying how you can provide value. Your objective is to identify what's stopping them from achieving what they want. There are two approaches:

1. If you've heard something during the fact finding where your offer fits, probe further. Perhaps they've commented that they'd like to get their product to market faster, and you know that you can help with this.

2. If, during the fact finding, you've not found a clue about where your product might add value, ask an open question relating to what you can offer, e.g. "What would you like to improve in your current situation in relation to your employees who are remote working?"

R stands for **Repercussion**. You've identified where you can add value and now you want to big up the pain by helping them visualise the repercussions of the obstacle. Get them to paint a picture (not literally unless, they're into that) with questions like:

- How does this impact your results?
- How much additional cost does that mean for your department?
- What would it mean to you personally if you could fix this?

Patience is critical at this stage as, the greater the need you create, the more convincing you'll be when presenting the solutions.

Some straws: Your first meeting

- Clear your mind of your company, products and services every time you seek to understand. Focus on the customer, not your stuff.
- Listen to understand, not to reply.
- When you identify a solution, don't get overexcited and start to sell. Ask more questions to make the client's need bigger.

CHAPTER 9:

Following up and keeping up momentum

What's this about?

In this section you'll learn about two skills that you'll need to keep deals moving: keeping up the momentum, and following up.

All about momentum

In sales, momentum is forward motion. It's keeping:

- Your prospect interested in you.
- The sales process moving forward, by being proactive and exact with your prospect in taking the next step.

It usually means that you're keeping your calls and visits linked i.e. at the end of a call you've made definite plans to visit your prospect. Or at the end of a visit you've agreed you'll call in two weeks.

Keeping up momentum is different from following up. Following up is staying visible to your prospect when there's no definite meeting or call arranged.

Why is keeping up momentum important?

Getting a prospect interested in what you have to sell can be easy in the initial stages, but initial interest is a long, long way from getting them to sign on the dotted line. There are many reasons for this, but one major factor is that the potential buyer loses interest in you and what you're selling. It's not a priority for them. This is why it's important for you to manage the process of keeping them interested.

Momentum starts from the first interaction you have with your client, and, in our experience, if you keep the momentum going, it speeds up the sales process so you'll make a sale morc quickly.

You can measure the momentum theory yourself by splitting your closing ratio by time. Here's a real-life example from a sales team we worked with:

- Closing ratio of deals that took less than 25 days to work on — 69%
- Closing ratio of deals that took more than 25 days to work on — 16%

The team were surprised but, in real life, it's just sort-of physics. Momentum keeps things in motion. If you're in motion, you'll get to your goal faster. But keeping the momentum going isn't just about getting a deal faster. In our experience, keeping the momentum going means:

- You'll secure lots more meetings at the right time.
- You'll understand more about your client's interest levels more quickly. If they're really not interested, it's better to find out early on.
- You'll uncover more information that could help with the future sale.

What does lost momentum look like?

Oh, it looks bad. You might be very confident that you'll close a deal, but here are the warning signs that momentum has left the room. Things go quiet. Delays started to happen. You take your eye off the ball, focussing on other clients. In the end, you lose that piece of business. It just drifts away. Why? Because you lost momentum.

How to keep momentum

Keeping momentum uses your following up skills to the full. Here are some ways to keep momentum going:

- Set your next meeting during your last contact with the customer. Be precise. Don't say "I'll call you next week to set up another meeting" , because it's easy to lose touch and difficult to get back on track again. If you're with your customer, they'll be more inclined in the moment to meet with you again, but this will wear off over time.

- If a customer contacts you, or you have met them at an event, fix a date there and then to meet.
- Create reasons why you need the next steps to be sooner than later: offers, deadlines, the time of the year. As long as the reason is plausible (and real, obviously!) little pushes can keep the momentum going well.
- If there's been a delay in the sale and you feel that the gap between meetings is too long, create a useful reason to see the client, to keep you top of mind and their interest alive.

Can you stop with the momentum when you're about to make the sale?

Six words for you. Are you out of your mind?

We've sat on our butts basking in the glory of assuming we've made a sale, and it didn't end well.

It's easy to lose momentum just at the point of triumph. You need to stay focussed, even when you get the good news that a client is just about to sign up to your amazing product. But keep the momentum going. So, when a client tells you:

- That they are just getting the final sign off,
- That they will confirm in the morning, or
- Any other piece of information that tells you the deal is going to happen

don't spend your not-yet-earned bonus on that super new sewing machine because you're not there yet. You haven't won the deal. Yet. You need to act on the good news and close the deal immediately. You do this by keeping up the momentum by gently shoving your client to the next step by being exact. Assist in helping the client set their agenda.

For example, if the client says, "We'll be signing it off in the morning", respond with "Great, let's meet after you have done this at 2pm to get things moving". If they say, "I need to go over the pricing", you can respond "Great, so if you get that done tomorrow, let's meet the next day to discuss your review".

A straw: Keeping up momentum

For every interaction that you have with a potential client, always have an objective to set up and diarise the next activity.

All about following up

In sales, following up is any action you take after any contact with a prospect, potential customer, actual customer or even unqualified lead. Follow ups can be an action you take independently of your contact, or actions agreed with them. In this section we'll look at when during the sales process you'll need to follow up.

Hint: pretty much all the time.

Following up is all about staying visible to your prospect, without being a pain in the butt. Staying visible builds rapport and relationships, and gains commitment.

Why is following up important?

It's important because, in our experience, the more you follow up, the greater your chance of making that sale. The vast majority — around 80% — of sales are made between the 5th and the 12th contact. Sounds like stalking, but it's not. 'Contact' could mean any touch point — an email sending something useful, an invite to an event, a holiday greetings card at holiday time etc.

Why don't salespeople follow up?

If following up is important, why don't salespeople do it as much as they should?

Two words. Assumptions. Rejection.

Mostly, salespeople don't follow up because of assumptions they make, and because rejection hurts. In our experience:

- Salespeople that never follow up with a prospect assume that if the prospect wanted what they were offering, they would have said "yes, please" straight-away. They believe that no means no, and that following up is not going to convince them to change their mind.

- Salespeople that stop after one or two follow ups often assume that if the client didn't respond to them, or they felt fobbed off, the client will never buy. This is just an assumption. The client really could be busy. Life is wiggly. You're not their priority and real world stuff happens. So don't give up yet.
- Very few salespeople make three or more follow-up contacts because they understand how following up can increase their sales. They avoid making assumptions, and they are comfortable with rejection. They also make sure that their follow ups add quality or value, and are not just whiny emails.

When to follow up

Following up isn't just about keeping in touch with your client after you've given them an awesome proposal. Following up happens at each stage of the sales process.

Follow up when:

- You're trying to get to meet somebody for the first time. Usually you'll need to give it a few goes. Unless they've actually said, "Go away, I never want to hear from you ever again. Ever," then it's always worth another attempt within a reasonable amount of time. It's your call. Maybe a week later, maybe a year later. You'll know what's right.
- You've met with the customer and they've agreed to do something, such as have a second meeting, give you more information or introduce you to somebody else in

their organisation. They've agreed to it, and at the time they might have meant it, but it's not always the case that it happens unless you follow up a couple of times.

- You want to stay in touch with customers that have initially rejected you. This is all part of the fun of recycling opportunities or identifying future new opportunities.
- You want to keep in touch with your existing clients. They might have a soft spot for you but you're not the centre of their world, so you may have to follow up on your offers or suggestions a couple of times.
- You want to meet new contacts within your existing client base. Perhaps you've been introduced, directly or indirectly, but you'd like to make sure of a meeting or whatever objective it is you're after.
- You've provided your awesome solution and want to close the deal.

This list won't break records but it does cover the more usual situations where you'll want to practise your shiny following up skills.

Don't trust your brain to make sure you follow up at the right time. Make sure you've set reminders in your CRM or activity planner. If you do, and follow up at the right time, you'll land in that 10% of high performers and will be far more successful than the average salesperson. Don't get too smug, though.

How to follow up without being a pain in the butt

Deciding when to follow up is pretty straightforward, as long as you know the definitions of stalking or harassing. Following up is neither of these, and not is it becoming a pain in the butt to your customer.

Non-weird following up involves:

1. Understanding that you're not the centre of your prospect's world.

It would be weird if you were. Hopefully you've made a positive impact, but they'll have other priorities on their plate. If they don't answer your call or email, don't take this as an outright rejection. What you're offering will be more important to them sometimes, and less at other times.If they don't respond it doesn't necessarily mean that they have no interest.

2. Staying a little more visible than your competitors

Sit back with a cup of tea and imagine that you're selling to somebody who has an existing supplier but they're looking at alternatives. You've presented your amazingly useful solution and you think it went well. By following up, you're staying visible with your prospect, but you're also putting pressure on their current supplier. The more professional your follow up, the further ahead of your competition you will be. By staying a little more visible or helpful than their current supplier, your chances of winning the beauty contest just increased.

3. Making it easy for your prospect.

If you're helpful and professional in your follow-ups, you make it easier for your prospect to choose you, rather than go back through all the other proposals. If they have all the information they need, there's a clear link between what you're offering and their business need, and you seem like a decent company, then it's much easier for them to say yes to you than go back through a ton of other proposals. Put it on a plate for them.

4. Thinking about their budgets.

Your prospect will probably have stuff that's competing for cost. Let's say they need a new phone system and a computer system upgrade, but they've only got the budget for one of them. It's more likely that the salesperson who's kept themselves visible with their consistent follow-up will have a better chance of getting a sale.

Following up without following up

Following up without following up is staying in contact with your client with stuff that they might find useful or interesting. The beauty of this is that you're never a pain to your potential client. You're giving them something (hopefully) useful to them, and, in doing so, showing that you understand what they need or where their interests lie. And, for potential customers, it's so much more fun receiving something interesting than a voice saying: 'Any news on the proposal, yet?" You're not asking for business, and you're keeping yourself in your potential client's mind. In our experience, when we've sent an article that links to a conversation we've had with our client, they've proactively replied, referring to the 'deal on the table' quite often.

It really works.

Follow up communication methods

You've a lot of choice with this one: the right one for you is the right one for your prospect. Which method of contact do they prefer? It won't take you long to realise that one client never replies to your emails or answers their phone, but always texts you back. Or they never reply to your text but late evenings they respond to your email.

If you're not sure, here are some pros and cons:

Phone

Yes, this old-fashioned method is key to getting more of a commitment from the client. When you have a real conversation, it's two-way and interactive, so you've the opportunity to explore issues live. In our experience phone calls are effective, second only to in-person meetings.

Email

Email can be the best way to follow up, especially as people are becoming too busy to answer their phone. Email gives your client the opportunity to check it out at a time that's convenient to them and to answer when they want.

Whatsapp

In our experience, there's a perception that, because WhatsApp is free, it's a 'cheap' and informal way to communicate. We would never use this with new customers but if you're contacted first by WhatsApp then it's fine to use. As with text messaging, too, don't drag out a text message. Keep focussed.

Dropping in to see the client

Erm. Stalking, much? Be very careful here. You don't want a restraining order put on you. The only time you drop in unannounced is if the client has given you a definite, authentic, real invitation to drop in. However, even in this situation it's polite to check if it's ok to pop in. You'll still need an objective, and something useful to offer. You're not there to drink their tea and chat about the weather.

Peter's story: How to follow up without following up

I was invited to speak at a conference for a global company (yay, me!) and met the CEO. We had a good chat about how it's important for salespeople to learn the fundamentals of sales without the fuss. He told me he'd like me to have an ongoing relationship with his company's sales teams across the world. I thought "Whoop, well done me!"

I left it for a week and followed up with an email. I got a reply the next day. It was very polite but it also had a clear message for me not to follow up, and that he would come back to me when he was ready. I was left in a spot now. I knew I had to follow up, but I had been given a very clear message not to. Any follow up now would make me look rude, and be disrespectful to the CEO.

About three weeks later I remembered an article that I had written for a trade magazine about a year earlier. It was mega-relevant to what the CEO and I had discussed. I sent it to the CEO and mentioned that I thought it might be helpful to his sales team. Nothing salesy, no mention at all about following up on the big opportunity. I got a reply instantly. It was a simple note to say, "Can we set up a call to finalise our ongoing relationship?" Everything went smoothly from there.

The moral of this story is that if you're useful, you can follow up anytime.

Some straws: Momentum and following up

- Make sure that your sales system includes space and time for following up, so that it becomes a regular part of the process.
- Don't be that salesperson who annoys the hell out of the prospect. Be useful and professional.

CHAPTER 10:

Developing a persuasive selling statement

What's this about?

In this section you'll find out how to put together the words and ideas that will persuade your customers to buy from you.

What's a persuasive selling statement?

A persuasive selling statement is the chunk of words you use that helps your prospect take the next right step. This could be anything from buying that thing you sell right there and then, to arranging a meeting with some higher-ups for a bigger sale. It's not going to be the same every time, because no two situations are the same, but there are three commonalities:

Your statement will:

1. Link what you offer to your prospect's needs.

2. Demonstrate the impact of what you're offering on your prospect's needs.
3. Use your prospect's business language.

Why is a persuasive selling statement important?

It's important because it makes your prospect understand exactly how what you're offering makes things better for them, and is articulated in such a way that it's very difficult to turn down. It's not exactly an offer they can't refuse — you won't be using horses' heads in your repertoire, but it's an offer that is very easy for them to accept.

How to develop a persuasive selling statement

If you've completed the questioning stage correctly, you'll have gathered together a whole feast of opportunities where what you sell can really, really, really help them. So exciting! So — why didn't they buy anything from you?

There are two common reasons.

1. You've talked about your company and what it can do, and assumed that your prospect has linked what you've said to their business. They haven't.
2. You've explained what the impact on their business might be, but failed to show how what you're offering makes the impact.

So, how do you make sure your offer is clearly linked to what your prospect is looking for, demonstrates how it makes an impact, and uses your prospect's business language?

Yes...it's that old chestnut: Features, advantages and benefits (FABs).

It's an old chestnut because it works. You craft your selling statement using:

- The features of what you're selling.
- The advantages to the prospect of these features.
- The benefits on your prospects' business that these advantages create.

Let's take a look.

What's a feature?

A feature is a specific characteristic of your organisation or of what you're offering. It's a fact, not an opinion and not an assumption.

Let's play a game called Feature or Not Feature?:

We've been in the business for 60 Years. Feature or not feature?

Yes, this is a feature. It's specific and it's a fact. If you've been in business for 60 years it sounds like your organisation is good at what it does.

Our organisation is good at what it does. Feature or not feature?

Nope. This is just an opinion. Can you see the difference? Can you also see the assumptions that can be made from a feature? Interesting, huh?

It has an in-built voice recorder. Feature or not feature?

Yes. It's a specific characteristic of the product. This is an easy one.

We have a presence in many countries. Feature or not feature?

Nope. It sounds like a feature but "many" has different interpretations. If you're a start-up and selling in six countries, that might feel like "many" to you. But to your prospect, whose company sells in 154 countries, it's not. They could feel that you've misled them, making you sound bigger than you are. (Even if you think you're big).

If you sell in five countries and they happen each to be in a different continent then having a presence in five continents is technically a feature.

We are the best in the business. Feature or not feature?

No. Just opinion, and it never sounds convincing.

We have a 95% accuracy rate. Feature or not feature?

Yes. This is a feature, and a powerful one for your selling statement.

Our customers love us. Feature or not feature?

Nope. Just an opinion. You may have some evidence e.g. an "I love you" card from three of your customers, but unless you have evidence from every single customer, generalising doesn't make it accurate. Or a feature.

Use evidence to turn opinion into features. If your company or product has won awards e.g. for customer service, good design or eco-friendliness – then, if you think these aspects are important to your prospect, use them as features. If your product has good market share, use this as social proof.

What's an advantage?

Here's where you can let your opinions run riot. Advantages are the key points of a feature that help your prospect understand the story of impact you can have on their business. Advantages:

- Help piece together your selling statement.
- Builds towards the benefit.
- Links the thing the feature does to the impact on your prospect's business needs.
- Helps explain the feature more – this helps especially if the feature is particularly technical and your prospect isn't.
- Makes your selling statement more exciting.

Don't get features and advantages mixed up. We often see salespeople add another feature to their original feature e.g. "We have a 24 hour operation with access to over 150,000 line items". 24 hour operations and access to 150,000 line items are both features, but many salespeople would sell the 150,000 as an advantage. The actual advantage would be something like, "which means you can receive any item you are looking for at any time day or night".

There may be several advantages to one feature. As you build an advantage on to another advantage, you build the story.

What's a benefit?

A benefit sounds like it might be an advantage, but it isn't. A benefit is a specific impact on your prospect's business.

Let's look at what we might think of as a benefit: "to save time". This isn't a benefit because we don't know if or how it impacts your prospect's business. How much time is saved? What will they do with the saved time? What will the impact be to their business? The answers to these questions will be the benefit. The benefit defines your offer.

See how it works in practice:

Example: You're selling paper cups to two different prospects:

1. Low-cost restaurant

Feature: The cups are made of paper

Advantage: Paper cups don't break

Benefit: Your prospect is currently losing USD 450 per month in broken china cups. The clientele doesn't care what it drinks from, so using paper cups will save money.

2. Nursery

Feature: The cups are made of paper

Advantage: Paper cups don't break

Benefit: Eliminates breakages, which can harm the children and affect the nursery's reputation.

You'll see that features and advantages are the same, but the benefits are different because they relate to separate impacts on the prospects' business.

How it all fits together with the FOR and USE questioning techniques

Understanding and **fact finding** usually uncover the required **feature**.

The **specifics** or **obstacles** normally uncover the **advantages**.

The **repercussions** or **enlarging** identify the **benefits**.

How to say your persuasive selling statement without sounding like a robot

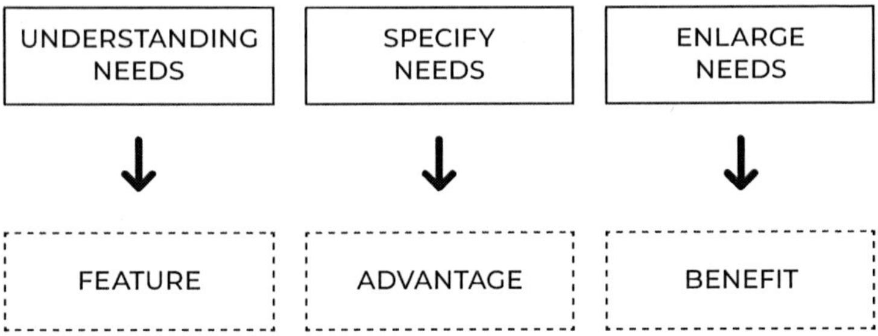

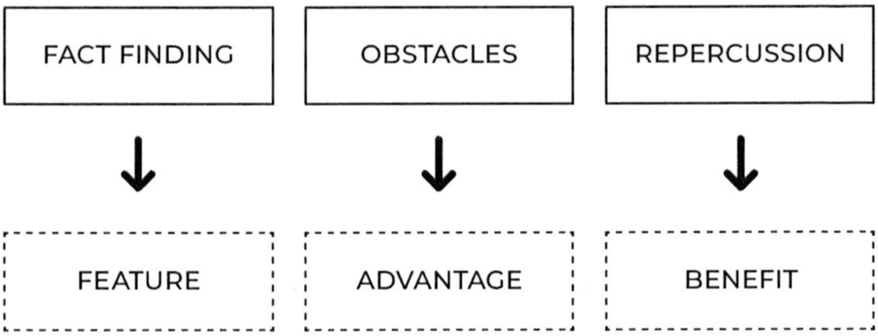

The golden phrase is "which means that...". This links your features, advantages and benefits. In practice your statement:

a) Starts with a feature.

b) Ends with a benefit.

c) Uses "which means that" (the golden phrase, remember?) to link it all together.

E.g. "Our customer service is 24 hours which means that you can have questions answered day or night. This means that your night duty staff can stay on target, rather than take that hour of downtime each shift ,which you say is costing you £x in lost productivity. "

Some straws: Developing a persuasive statement

- Be driven by your prospect's needs, not by what you have to sell.
- Create your Features/Advantages/Benefits flow for each prospect.
- Only choose features that relate to your prospect's business needs. Don't choose your own or what you think is popular.
- If you're confused about how to sell something, it means you need more information. Ask your prospect more questions.

CHAPTER 11:
Presenting solutions

What's this about?

You'll find out the different kinds of ways to present solutions, and we'll do a deep dive into in-person solution presentations, because these are the scariest.

In-person presentations are often the quicksand within the sales process – the prospect's will to buy from you will sink without trace if you don't get it right. We've found that many sales people are poor at presentation and presenting solutions, so, if you do it well, you'll skyrocket the difference between other salespeoples' success and yours.

An in-person presentation takes up your prospect's valuable time – so you must make your presentation valuable.

Why is presenting solutions correctly important?

If you don't present your solution clearly, you'll have wasted all that hard work up to now: finding a prospect, identifying the right person to meet, getting that meeting, questioning your prospect in order to understand them. When you present your solution effectively, your prospect clearly understands how what you're offering helps them.

Do presenting solutions effectively always mean an in-person presentation?

No, it doesn't. It all depends on your circumstances. If you're selling a pack of pencils, nope. If you're selling a ten-year contract for supplying all the pencils to a large conglomerate, then we would say yes.

How to package your solution

Solutions can be packaged differently – in the form of a verbal price offer, a written quote, a written in-depth proposal or an in-person presentation. But they must all show clearly how what you're offering addresses your prospect's business need.

Should you offer a price after you've questioned your prospect?

During your meetings you've used good questioning techniques and you've uncovered the pain or the gain for your prospect. Unless you're utterly sure that you can close the deal there and then, put some more value on the table. If you offer the price immediately at the end of asking your questions, the prospect may think that they're part of your factory — that you offer the same solution to everybody, that nothing was tailor made and that, no matter what they had told you, you would have offered the same product or service. How special do they feel? Not.

A good way to end the meeting here would be to confirm the key points to show that you've understood, and then to ask if you can come back another time to present your tailored solution to them. You can mention that you need to complete some checks in order to provide an accurate offer.

Quotes v proposals

A quote is just about numbers. If you provide a number (price) for what you're offering, without clarifying the solution further or differentiating what you're offering from your competitors, your prospect is likely to compare numbers and go with the cheapest. Is your product or service the cheapest in the market? Probably not.

By calling your solution a quote you're telling the client that it is just about price, and that they should ignore any value.

Proposals are really just "My awesome solution for your business needs, and, P.S. here's how much it costs." **Proposals should ooze value.** It's the solution itself, demonstrating how you can improve the client's position by addressing their needs and eliminating their problems. Yes, you need to bung in the price, but load up on the value. Your prospect will always weigh up and compare the value against the price to see if they believe it is worth it. It's your job to make sure the value outweighs the price in every proposal.

How about if you just email them your proposal?

Common, but dangerous. You've spent time putting together an awesome proposal, and you've hit send. But most prospects will open the attachment and go straight to the pricing section. If they actually read the value sections, you're allowing the customer to interpret your offer for themselves, and you have absolutely no direct way of influencing their decision.

Why in-person presentations are important

1. More chance to add value

Any question your prospect asks is a chance for you to articulate more value and add to the persuasiveness of your offer. Here are some numbers to think about. We've found that:

- A prospect that you've emailed will ask three questions on average.
- A client you've called will ask seven questions on average.
- A prospect you're presenting to will ask 14 questions on average.

That's 14 chances to add value and more strongly influence your prospect.

Always try to present your proposal in person.

2. You can assess and influence the level of interest

It's a good sign if they've agreed to a further meeting with you — they're interested. But being actually in front of them, you're able to influence more people and control the flow and mood of the meeting. You can address your prospects' reservations (which you would probably never have found out about through email) and reassure them.

3. You can influence more people

If you've a mix of people at the presentation — the decision makers, the people who will use your solution, the accountants — you've a great opportunity to educate all the people with the buying power about the value you're offering firsthand.

There are of course practicalities. If your prospect is miles away (or if there's a global pandemic), it could be a big hassle (or immoral) to make the trip again. But video calls exist, so use them.

Presenting your solution: an overview

Cool! You've got a big fat "yes" to "Can I come back to go through my solution with you?". Well done! Here are our top tips:

1. It's your show. It's important that your presentation is your show. This means that you'll need to keep control of it. This doesn't mean you do all the talking or expect your audience to sit up and shut up. It's a two-way process, and the more your audience feels engaged, the better.

2. Don't talk about price until the end of your presentation.

3. Enjoy and use questions. Clients ask questions for two reasons:

- They need clarity.
- They're interested in how they might use what you're offering. Yay!

Your prospect's questions are important because they could flag up areas of value that, even with your best questioning and understanding of the client, you haven't thought of or didn't know about. You only find these areas out by presenting in-person — and that's why we bang on about how important presenting in-person is.

4. Find out why clients ask those questions

It's important to answer your prospect's question, but also find out why they asked it in the first place. The answer could be a goldmine for extra value you can offer, which you may have missed during your questioning. For instance, if your prospect asks about your product's carbon footprint, answer their question and follow up with questions about what's important to them about carbon footprint. It could be because they're very eco-conscious, or are scored on their own carbon footprint, or something else.

5. Be interactive

If you feel you are losing the room, ask a relevant question e.g. something that relates to their organisation or work practice. If there's a key message you want to get across to the audience, ask them what their thoughts are on any associated results first. For example, a digital media salesperson may want to highlight the number of people that Google search their client's industry. Before revealing the number, they will first ask their audience their opinion. This gets the prospect involved and linking the issue to their own business, and perks them up a bit.

6. Don't forget a strong 'close'

Always build in a 'close' or agreement on next steps into your presentation. Every contact with a client should always end with agreement on what happens next, and it's just the same for in-person presentations.

Presentations can be stressful, and it's no wonder that we've seen salespeople lose steam at this most important point. They're relieved that the presentation is over and want to exit the room as fast as possible. It's important to keep focused right until you have completed what you wanted to achieve and have left the client. Then you can sit in the car and eat chocolate.

Creating the visuals for your presentation

Society has come a long way from those mind-numbing 70-slide presentations, and we couldn't be more delighted.

When you're putting together the visuals that will illustrate your proposal, remember to put yourself in your prospect's position. Do they care about your company's 300 year old history? Probably not.

If you have three relevant slides in a deck of 400, those three will drown.

You may have produced a beautiful presentation that you would guard with your life, but if much of it isn't actually relevant to your prospect, ditch it. Murder your darlings.

Peter's story: What not to do

We were in a meeting with a salesperson who was presenting his solution. He had 56 slides and it was obvious he didn't think all of them were important. So, when he lost interest in a slide, he said 'This isn't important' or 'Let's skip these slides and move on to the next'. He lost the room. If they're not important to him, why should they be important to his audience? People started to look at their phones or whisper to their neighbours. When he became motivated again with the next relevant slide, the majority of the room was not with him. They were still on their phones or chatting, so he never got any of his key messages across. The interesting part of this was that he was quite unaware of it, until we had a conversation afterward. He was too focused on saying what he had to say, rather than delivering a clear and concise message to an audience, and checking with them that they were engaged and into it.

So make sure that your presentation is chock full of how what you do can help their business, and this means a dive into the features, advantages and benefits that you've already discovered. Less is more.

The presentation's title

Pack it with value. Make it interesting and useful. It should give any person who's casually wandered into the room an overview of how your company or product helps their company.

So, "Our proposal for Prospect X"? Nope.

How about:

"Increasing brand exposure for Prospect X across the MENA." That's ok, if everyone knows what MENA means.

"Make your customers love you more": Warm, emotive, not specific, but definitely interesting.

"Improving Company X Workforce Efficiency"

The title needs to be relevant and illustrate that you've listened to them during the questioning meeting.

The hook

The hook is something that'll make your audience sit up and think, "This is going to be good. They get me. It's gonna be about my challenges/ambitions/big problems."

The hook is a fact, statistic or quotation that has real impact, such as "100% of companies that implemented this improvement plan grew their sales by more than 20%, with no additional cost in the sales team. "

This may be optional and depends on the industry, the product or service and the environment.

The main content

You'll remember that less is more, so it's time to pack as much value in as few slides as possible. It's hard work, but it's worth it. Create the story that will lead them to the conclusion, in slide form.

Slides should contain:

- A maximum of 20 words. It's not an essay.
- A maximum of four bullet points.
- Consistent fonts and sizes. Inconsistency is distracting and unprofessional.
- One point/issue per slide, so that people focus on what you want them to. Building the points also helps you keep control of the narrative, even if you are distracted by questions or clarifications.

Don't forget — you've done well

- You've made the effort and taken the time to find the right opportunities for you to sell to.
- You've managed to get a meeting with the right person.
- You made a great first impression, gathered all the right information and have come up with a great solution.

So don't waste your hard work: spend quality time creating a professional presentation that will persuade your prospect to buy.

Some straws: presenting your solution

- Work hard to get an in-person presentation meeting, to present your proposal to the right audience.
- Prepare the presentation with as few slides as possible.
- Focus on telling the story that links what you're selling to the impact on your prospect's business.

CHAPTER 12:
Closing business

What's this about?

In this section you'll learn what closing business is, and the different types of closing you can use to take you further towards winning the deal.

What does closing business mean?

Closing business is asking your prospect to buy what you're offering. You'll also hear it called "closing the sale'.

In our experience, It's the number one area in which a salesperson can improve their performance. Time and time again we see salespeople pull back from the simple act of asking for the prospect's business. Asking for business increases your results, so our advice is just do it. Every time.

But we recognise that it's not easy. It can feel uncomfortable. So in this section we'll look at what might stop us from closing the sale, and we'll also look at how closing is so vital at a number of stages during the "making the sale" process.

Why is closing business important?

When you're in front of your prospect and have clearly outlined your offer, you're in your most persuasive position. If you capitalise on this moment as best you can, you'll at least gain an advantage — if not the signed deal. Otherwise, your chances decrease and you could open the door to your competitors and also invite in other priorities that could hinder your progress.

Why don't salespeople ask for business?

Hmm. Difficult one. With our shared 70 years in sales, you'd think we'd have the answer to this one, but it's tricky. Aren't salespeople supposed to enjoy the thrill of the chase? Aren't all salespeople outgoing confident types? Isn't the excitement of closing business what it is all about?

Possibly.

Debatable.

We think that because salespeople are people, too (believe it or not), their reasons for not closing are as individual as they are. We've found that:

- Some feel that there's a social stigma attached to actually asking for the business. It's just not polite.
- Some aren't trained to ask for the business. It's as if by magic their prospect will say. "Ooh, lovely, yes please," without them having to ask.
- Some are worried about rejection. They may take it personally, or they may not know how to deal with a 'no'.
- Some feel that the stakes are too high — they view the close is the end result of all their hard work, and that a rejection in person might tip them over the edge.
- Some are worried that the prospect might react badly — "You're pushy, aren't you?" "Woah, there, tiger, slow down a bit."

But if you understood the massive positive impact that closing every time at the completion of your proposal has on your overall figures, you'll be closing like a maniac.

We've found that the prospect will not bite your head off. And when you've learned how to handle objections, getting a 'no' isn't a kick in the butt: it's just an opportunity to practise handling objections.

Here's more good news: you don't need any special knowledge or added skills to close. It's down to confidence and the understanding that closing is just another part of your sales role.

Let's talk about the buying line

The buying line is the same as the finish line in a race. It's the point at which your prospect will agree to your proposal. With every interaction with them, you're moving them nearer to the buying line.

The downside? The moment that you leave the meeting or sales pitch, most prospects will retreat further away from the buying line for one reason only — they get distracted. Their distraction pushes your solution further down their list of priorities.

This is what it looks like:

You've just had a blast of a meeting with your prospect, and you skip off like a pixie back to the office, to tell your boss how great it went. While this is happening, your prospect grabs a cuppa and thinks, "Yes, I liked what that salesperson was saying. I think we'll go ahead." But then:

- She opens her email and she's overwhelmed at her packed-to-exploding inbox.
- She opens her email and finds a metaphorical fire that needs to be put out immediately.
- She's hungry and thinks about lunch.
- Somebody enters her office and says she is needed urgently.
- Her husband phones and says the kids are playing up again. She spends ten minutes after sorting it all out, wondering if couples counselling would be useful.

Distractions happen because prospects are people. Life happens and life does not care if you've just performed the best presentation in the history of presentations.

That's why it's important to close while you are with your prospect, in person.

Why being straightforward works

- When you're about to ask for your prospect's business, you might be tempted with a 'soft' close. Soft closes look something like this:
- So, what do you think?
- Is it something you are interested in?
- Does this look good to you?

These questions put your prospect in control of the next steps. It's easy for them to say:

- Just give me some time to think about it and I'll get back to you.
- Yes, I'm interested; just give me some time and I'll discuss it with my team, and I'll come back to you.
- Yes, it looks good to me. Let me see how we can move forward, and I'll be in touch.

Whoops! You've just lost momentum in the sale and it could be difficult to get things back on track because it's much much harder to redirect them by phone or email later. They're slipping back from the buying line. So, ask for their business outright. Look them in the eye and ask, "Have we a deal?"

If you get a ‘no’, don’t panic, because a no can be good. You have clarity. You know where you stand. And now you have an objection to handle while you’re there in front of your prospect.

You’ll find out one of two things, and either is good. You’ll find out:

- What you need to do to win the business, or
- It’s a permanent objection, so the prospect will never buy from you. You don’t need to spend more time on this prospect.

Gaining a ‘no’ and having the opportunity to talk through the objection with your prospect is better than leaving the meeting without being sure of what is happening next.

Getting a no: here’s where you can improve

Why do a lot of deals not close?

If you’re getting too many rejections, it’s not always because your prospect can’t understand what’s good for them. It’s likely that they’re saying no because of deficits or gaps in your sales process. Something’s gone wrong on the way to the close. Maybe:

- Your prospect wasn’t the right target market.
- You weren’t talking to the right person.

- You didn't build rapport in the early stages or didn't gain trust.
- You lost momentum during the sale.
- You didn't understand the customer well enough.
- You didn't clearly link what you were offering to a positive impact on the prospect's business.
- The prospect felt that you were unreliable at some point.

Your prospect isn't likely to give you detailed feedback (and why should they? They don't owe us anything) so it's worth reviewing your process, and adding straws in so that you become the best you can be. That's all you can ask of yourself.

Gaining commitment is closing, but different.

Gaining commitment is closing, but a different type of closing. Gaining commitment is asking your prospect not to buy the thing, but to do something else that you know will get them nearer to the buying line. It's a way of keeping the momentum going.

Gaining commitment could be:

- Asking for the next meeting.
- Asking for some information.
- Asking for an introduction.
- Asking them to visit your office / plant / location.
- Asking for your boss to meet with their boss.
- Asking to introduce your technical or operational team.

Often there is a point in the sales process where, once you achieve your objective, the rest of the sale falls into place. Something 'unlocks.'It could be a meeting with a key person that gains trust, or finding the information that demonstrates how you can add massive value. Or something else. But you'll know it when you see it.

Ways of asking for commitment

When you want to direct your prospect to a particular answer, use closed questions, where they can only answer yes or no, or alternatives, where they can choose options, but none of the options are "No thanks".

The Alternative Close: Provide two choices, and if either is agreed to, you've gained the commitment. Example: Would you like to meet today or tomorrow?

The Direct Close: Simply asking straight out for the commitment. Example: Would you like to come to our facility to see how we operate?

The Assumptive Close: Assume that they're convinced and fine with you moving ahead to the next logical step of the sale. Example: When would you like me to come back and present some solutions to the problems we've been discussing?

The Negotiation Close: This may require some strategy, but if you're prepared, it can work well.

Example 1: If you arrange for me to meet with your technical team, let's do it around lunchtime and I'll bring pizza."

Example 2: If we can make a time with your MD, I'll make sure my MD is also present."

Peter's story: Change the objective

I was working with a company that made exhibition stands and we identified an amazing statistic. If a potential client visited their super-impressive joinery, their closing ratio increased to 90%. Gaining commitment was critical.

This changed the sales team's objective. We took the focus away from closing deals. The new objective was "Get the prospect to the joinery." Although with a threefold increase in footfall the closing ratio dropped quite quickly from 90% to 60%, however, with three times the number many, many more deals were closing and sales were up.

Some straws: Closing business

- Always directly ask for the business after you've provided the solution. A 'no' can be managed.
- Keep gaining commitment to set objectives throughout the sales process.
- Create a checklist to ensure you've done everything before you try and close.

CHAPTER 13:
Handling objections

What's this about?

In this section you'll learn the difference between permanent and temporary objections; why objections are your new best friend, and how to respond to them.

Why objections are good

Objections are a good way of finding out the truth about our prospect's position. We use them to develop solutions and our relationship with these future customers. They're also good practice in managing our own emotional responses to rejection and our resilience and ingenuity in overcoming them.

About objections

Not every client says yes. Anything but a yes is an objection.

Selling is (and should be) the only part of life where no doesn't necessarily mean no.

We've distinguished between the "no's" that mean "no" and the "no's" that mean "possibly" like this:

Permanent objection: A no that means "No" "No way" or even "Get out, now." This client will never, ever buy from you. Ever. Don't even. Nope.

Temporary objection: A no that means "No, but maybe I don't have the right information/power/understanding to say yes at the moment."

A temporary objection is still an objection. It's your right to offer. It's your client's right to object, and you have to respect that, but the temporary objection is the objection that you can work on, to get to a friendly 'yes' more effectively. You'll do this by:

- Distinguishing more quickly between permanent and temporary objections.
- Using a structure to identify, take apart and solve temporary objections.

Why is it important to handle objections effectively?

Hands up who likes to spend a whole lot of time, brainpower and energy on customers who are never, ever, ever going to buy from you.

Thought as much.

Chasing after clients who will run as soon as you set foot in their door is a waste of their time and yours.

This means you can focus your time and cleverness on working on the objections that you can actually overcome. Hopefully, if you've been working on showing the client how what you offer can solve his most urgent business need, you'll reduce the number of objections you get.

How to handle objections

Clients will have objections to what you're offering. Don't cry because this is sales life. Some of the objections will be fair, and some of them will be unfair. It's not up to you to judge. It's a waste of time and energy getting your underwear in a twist because you think you've been treated badly. Most salespeople have been rejected by a customer after months of following up. It's just part of the job. An icky part, maybe, but it's character building and you're gonna build your character so big by the end of this book.

But there are three things that are up to you:

1. To learn whether you've contributed to the "No, thanks", and what you can do about it for next time.
2. To decide if the objections are permanent and can ever be overcome.
3. To make sure that you can overcome objections that you decide aren't permanent.

Why clients say no but don't tell you the real reason

From our experience, many clients raise objections and they're not always truthful about it. How often do you hear a client say, "Thanks for your proposal and quote, but we had absolutely no intention of going with you guys because we'd planned on hiring my buddy in Company X for the job, but we needed three quotes to be compliant with our company buying policy. Thank you and goodbye." ?

Not often.

Here's why clients raise objections, and don't tell you the real reason:

- The three-quote policy.
- They're not the real decision maker.
- They may have a vested interest in buying from your competitors.
- They feel guilty or embarrassed about telling you the real reason.
- Meeting suppliers makes them feel important. Bless them.

We often give permanent objections ourselves, under cover of little white lies. It's because we're all human, and it's part of maintaining respectful social connections.

For instance, you're in a shop and have picked up some cool shoes. You're looking for the "These shoes are cool and totally vegan" label that you need, because you like animals and don't want to wear them. Uh-o, the label says, "These cool shoes are made of coolness but also bits of cow," so you know you'll never, ever buy them. As you're placing the now not-cool shoes back on the shelf, the sales assistant lurks up and asks, 'Can I help you?'. Instead of saying "No way am I buying these shoes made of cows. I feel nauseous and need to sit down," you'll say, 'No thanks, I'm just looking." You'll probably even give them a wan, pathetic smile.

Of course, if you'd been truthful you might have influenced a new line of non-cow-based cool shoes, but that's not how we act in the moment.

Distinguishing between permanent and temporary objections

Here's a six-step structure to play with, when handling objections. Like most things in sales, they're not foolproof, but they'll increase your chances of getting to yes, or at least to getting to move on to a more promising client sooner.

We'll use the common objection of "You're too expensive" in the structure. Let's say the cost of the lovely thing you're offering is USD 35,000.

Step 1: Acknowledge the objection

Acknowledging the objection shows that you've listened to them. It shows that you respect them (because you do, right?). Acknowledging the objection makes them feel comfortable about it. When they feel comfy, they're happier to open up about the objection and this gives you a way in to talk more about it. If you go into a strop, yelling about how on earth can they turn down this amazing offer, they'll throw you into the coffee machine, and rightly so.

But you don't want to admit that you're expensive. Say something soothing like, 'I understand that cost is important to everybody."

Step 2: The power question

Here's where you find out if the objection is permanent or temporary. Step two is asking one of the most powerful questions you can ask in sales:

'If we can resolve the issue of the price, will you sign the deal now?'

This is powerful because it's a way of flushing out the temporary objection, and you've not committed to reducing the price. If price is a temporary objection, they'll look you right in the eye and say 'Yes'. If they do a happy dance, it's a "YES!"

This means that they want to do business with you, so you can afford to get a little excited, but there's still work to be done.

Use the nature of the objection in the power question: it's not always price. For instance:

- If we can resolve the issue of the delivery dates, will you sign the deal now?
- If we can resolve the issue of the number of employees covered, will you sign the deal now?
- If we can resolve the issue of who'll be managing your account, will you sign the deal now?

If they answer "Yes, but…." it could still be a temporary objection, because they may need higher approval, or a compliance sign-off, to actually sign a deal, especially if it's a big one. But you're still in the game.

Step 3: Talking specifics

It's time to get more detail. So ask, 'When you say, 'too expensive', can you let me know just how much over cost we are?'

Let's say your client says, "I was hoping for something more like USD 28,000."

This gives you the actual figures to play with, Don't try to manage the objection without specifics.

Step 4: Focus on value

Now it's time to remember the final benefit of your FAB statement and bring in value. Link it to the difference they have just mentioned.

For instance, if your benefit can help them increase production to sell 3% more product, increasing sales of over 150,000 USD a month, ask them if this sounds worth spending the extra 1,250 USD. Don't mention the 35,000 USD, because a lower number sounds more appealing.

Step 5: Try the close again

Say: 'Are we ok to proceed?'

Step 6: Next steps

If they say yes, then you've done a good job. But if they're still hesitant, you've still done a good job because you have more information about the objection. If you feel that your client is actually interested, agree to go away and see what you can do. Before you leave, get another date in the diary.

Some straws: Handling objections

- Isolate the objection. Get the specifics.
- Practise the six steps to handling objections.
- Reflect on how you'd usually handle objections, and what difference the stepped process made.

CHAPTER 14:

Negotiating

What's this about?

In this section you'll learn the kinds of methods your potential client might use to get you to drop your price, and how to deal with them. We're not going to look at negotiation skills because, in the real world, even the best salespeople can't compete with procurement professionals in the art of negotiation. They'll spend 90% of their time negotiating, whereas for we salespeople, it's more like 10%.

Instead, we'll peek into the minds of our potential buyers to understand them better, and why they are negotiating. When we understand them more, we can be more confident in making our decisions about whether to drop our price, or not (usually, not). We'll also look at:

- Why discounts can really harm your profits.
- Why value is important.
- How to respond to the most common "give us a discount' ploys.

So, why not give them a discount?

We're not saying you should never give a potential buyer a discount. You may have been clever and added a buffer, knowing that a request for a discount was coming. Maybe you want to maintain a relationship, knowing there'll be more sales coming up. What we don't want to do is panic and lower our prices as soon as they ask us, because it's painful.

It's painful because of maths. Let look at it:

You sell your lovely thing for $100 and the cost to your company of your lovely thing is $80. Your customer wants a discount, so you offer to take off 10%. Just $10! That doesn't sound much. They can have it for £90.

But wait a minute! Your cost is still $80, so instead of a $20 profit, it's only $10 – which is a 50% drop in profit. Ouch!

If you repeat your discounts over and over, you'll lose an awful lot of profit.

A real-life cautionary tale

One of our sales trainees told us a story about how he created some new software that improved a production line output by 20%. He had no competitors. His buyer was stretched to the max and needed this improvement. His 20% improvement in productivity led to a 20% increase in sales, a profit margin for his client of hundreds of thousands of dollars.

Did he give a discount from his initial software price? He said "Yes, 10%. An insignificant number compared to the impact to their business and now I feel like an idiot."

Why do potential buyers negotiate?

1. They don't understand the value of your solution

Buyers are trained to negotiate and most focus only on price as the lever. Sometimes it's because they haven't understood the value you're offering. The only thing you need to remember when negotiating is that **if the other party talks price, you should talk value.**

Negotiating usually takes place after you have attempted to close the deal. By this stage you should have fully understood the client's needs. You'll already have outlined all the ways your solution provides them with value. Why discount further if you know that your solution will benefit them in other ways apart from the price?

The value you're offering might look like this:

- You're already saving them money on their costs for your product or service.
- Your solution is making an overall saving for their company.
- Your solution increases their production efficiency.
- They'll win more clients.
- They'll retain their clients.
- They'll save time.

- It makes their life easier.
- They can go home earlier.

It's important that you've foreshadowed the value of your solution, so that, at negotiation time, you've already stacked up the value to be obvious to the customer.

2. It's part of their procurement process

Buyers often try to negotiate the price down, even if they understand the value you're offering, because it's part of their procurement process. Trying for a discount, even when the value is understood, is very common.

You'll hear this a lot:

- I just don't have the budget.
- We don't have the budget to buy from you right now.
- Can you do something with the price?

Buyers are taught to use this as the first objection they bring up, because they're not saying an outright no, but it still puts pressure on us to drop the price. And sometimes we fold under pressure. In the words of a real buyer: "You know why it's so easy to get discounts with salespeople? They're just too desperate to get the deal closed'. And they're not wrong. Sometimes we are.

Common procurement strategies

We've met with a lot of different procurement strategies, and had conversations with lots of buyers who, strangely, were only too happy to share their strategies.

1. Getting a dirt cheap quote as a comparator to your offer

A buyer may have decided that they want to go with your offer, but will get another (much cheaper) offer from a company they have no intention of buying from. Just when you're sitting in front of them, ready to close the deal, they'll show you the offer with a flourish and say, "Hey, you really need to do something with your pricing, because look what I can get the deal for." If they're doing this, they're using you – and the other company.

Remember, it's just a ploy. Stand fast. Don't panic. Remember your value.

2. Being a total chancer

You'll have won the deal, or be very near to it. Maybe the contract's nearly up for signing. Then, out of the blue, one of the high-ups, maybe the CEO, will call you and say, "Yes, we want to go ahead but can you do anything about the price?" Cheeky, but it works because it's tempting for us, when we're so nearly there, to buckle and say, "Yes, no problem." Don't buckle because "being a chancer" is a procurement strategy.

Peter's story: The chancers

This happened to me twice within the space of three months: the same situation with both firms. I'd won a deal but, before being offered the contract, the CEO called me up and said he wanted to go ahead, but asked if there was anything I could do with the price. In both cases I started the usual,"Well, let's reflect on the value" chat, but before I got very far he stopped me and said, "It's fine, let's go ahead with your price."

I got to know both CEOs quite well, and I asked them why they had asked me to lower the price but didn't seem to want to discuss it. They both said the same thing: they did it with every deal and, more often than not, they got a discount. "You don't ask, you don't get!"

3. Starting a bidding war

This is very common, especially with online bidding where all the parties (buyer and suppliers) get bidding updates in realtime. So, a buyer puts you and four other companies into a bidding contest online, ostensibly to find the cheapest supplier. But don't get hooked – we've found that the cheapest offer is hardly ever the one selected by the buyer. And this is why: the buyer might have already selected the supplier they prefer. The bidding war is an effort to make them drop their price.

Bidding wars: Peter's story

My client was a supplier who had entered an online bidding war. They'd dropped their price a little, but then decided to back out. They knew their value, but they also knew their profit margin, and didn't want to erode it with a cheap offer. After they made the decision, they grabbed a coffee and watched their competitors battle it out online with bids that were getting lower and lower. After ten minutes, the phone rang. It was the head of procurement from the buyer, asking why they had stopped bidding. My client explained they could not go any lower than their latest price, and the conversation ended. Miraculously, the bidding stopped within five minutes and they received an email saying they had won the deal.

4. Just when you think it's over...

Many buyers will get what discount they can get from you and, when you're just about to settle the deal — so near closure — they'll say, "Oh, just one thing, there's someone else you need to meet," and the whole negotiating process starts all over again. The key here is to understand exactly who the decision maker is.

5. Procurement Key Performance Indicators

This isn't so much as procurement strategy, as something a buyer might be measured on by his managers. It's something to be aware of.

Peter's story: KPIs

I had won a large contract. It was all signed off by the managing director, and the sales director confirmed it was all going ahead. Yay! Five days later I got a call from their procurement department. They asked me for a meeting with the head of procurement to 'negotiate my contract'. I was puzzled but agreed to meet with them.

At the meeting I explained in a very nice way that I was not going to discount the price and that it would be crazy for me to do so. The head of procurement quietly agreed and acknowledged he had been late in being aware of the deal. He explained that he had an imaginary KPI jar, and that, when there was a new deal on the table, anything he could reduce from the chosen contract's initial proposal would go into this jar. For instance, if that proposal was 100, and he got it down to 90, 10 would be added to his KPI.

I learned to make sure I added an "imaginary jar" buffer to any sales offer with this company in future, so I could please everybody.

Sometimes procurement people need to show that they're providing value for their company, by getting discounts or something else of benefit. Throw them a bone. Add a buffer to your price, ready to use for a quick trade-off, if you think it's needed.

6. Surprise phone calls

If your buyer calls you to negotiate, they're all ready and prepared to give you all the reasons why they need a discount. Calls can catch you off-guard. You may not be prepared, and you need to be. Politely explain you'd be happy to meet up to talk about it as soon as possible. Then do your prep – value, non-financial discount choices etc – and prepare to close in that meeting.

Is there ever wiggle room?

Yes, of course there is. But not by giving buyers exactly what they want. If you think your offer through, you might find ways of giving away something that's not particularly of value to you, but it keeps the buyer happy.

Wiggle room: Peter's story

I had made an offer of my sales training programme to a client who said they loved it, it would be perfect – but my offer was not within their budget and that they only had 60% of what I was asking for. It seemed obvious that they wanted me to meet them in the middle, by reducing my price by 20%. But, because I'd done my homework about understanding their needs and that what I was offering would give them so much value, I was convinced that I had priced it fairly.

So I wrote them a friendly email back, stating that I, too, wanted to work with them, so I had some options for them:

1. *I'd reduce the price but I'd have to remove some of the content of the program. I didn't offer to remove the cheapest or most expensive elements, but what was of most value to them.*

2. *I wouldn't reduce the price but I offered them a deferred payment – don't pay now, pay later.*

3. *I offered to take 90% off an additional module (the smallest and least profitable module to me) if they kept the price as it was.*

The client accepted offer no. 3. Was I mad to give them a 90% discount? No, because I had achieved my goal of having them accept a price that was higher than they said they could afford. And the discount for the tiny module was far less than the 40% reduction they had been pushing for.

Sometimes offering options to buyers works well, if they think they're still getting a good deal, and it doesn't make your profit margin cry.

Draw up a list of non-financial discounts (discounts that won't affect your bottom line and you're perfectly happy to give away) to meet any price objections.

Some straws: Negotiating

- Always understand the needs and the improvements that your offer will bring. It's always about value. When prospects talk about price, you talk about value.

- Make sure you know who the decision maker is.
- Have your list of non-financial discounts ready.
- Turn negotiating phone calls into meetings, if you can.

CHAPTER 15:

Selling to existing customers

What's this about?

Whether you've made a sale to a customer for the first time, or you've had a customer on your books since the Cretacious, there's always more potential to make more sales.

Your customer base is a very rich resource that's right under your nose, but it's easy to take existing customers for granted. If you can create the mindset that your existing customers are actually new opportunities, you'll always be looking at how to add even more value to them, and make more sales in the process.

Why is selling to existing customers important?

Selling to existing customers can be classed as 'easy revenue' which sounds a bit insulting, but all it means is that you already have the relationship, the understanding of their business, and (hopefully) you've proved your company useful with previous sales. If you've gained their trust and proved your worth, it's easier to make a sale.

Lots of sales people focus on gaining new business rather than getting more from their existing customers — oops, big mistake. Generally, you have a much better chance of winning this business and improving your close ratio performance, too.

Here's why you should focus on selling to existing customers, in a bit more detail. (Just in case you need more convincing).

- The big deal is that you already have a relationship with them, and this means:
- It's easier for you to build an accurate profile.
- You can ask direct questions and get more accurate answers.
- You can leverage your past and existing positive dealings.
- Your brand is known (and hopefully liked) through the organisation.
- If one of your current contacts is the decision maker for the additional business, it strengthens your position further.
- If the decision maker isn't your current contact, you've already a contact in the organisation to help you make the introduction.
- An endorsement or recommendation from your current contact to a new contact within the organisation is social proof.

- You already understand the business, and this means you can offer a wider variety of valuable solutions.

Why are existing customers often overlooked?

If existing customers are such a crazy-good opportunity, why are they so ignored by sales people?

Overall, salespeople often assume that their clients are fully aware of all of the products and services that their company offers. Customers often expect their salesperson to understand their business and proactively provide information on whether there's a product or service that may suit what they need.

But there are other reasons:

- Lack of industry understanding: If you don't understand every aspect of your customers' business, then you'll not be able to match your products and services to what they really need.
- Customers may not be willing to offer up certain information. Whatever the reason for this may be, it's up to the salesperson to take the time and effort to build the relationship, to understand the customer and to find the information that they need.
- Your contact may not be aware of other opportunities for you in other parts of their own business. It's easy for people to be siloed in their organisation. They have so much to do. There's so much going on for them. Why

would they be thinking that what you're selling them might be great for their colleague Jo in Marketing, too?

How to sell to existing customers

It's our responsibility to make sure that we keep asking questions about our clients' business, to understand needs as they arise, and to proactively make sure that clients know about the products and services that can address their needs.

So, to effectively sell to existing customers:

1. View them as new opportunities, but also as a long-term relationship: see the lifetime value, not just the value of each individual sale.
2. Build up a profile: This means talking to the customer over time in their own language — not your industry jargon — and actively building a broad profile of the customer. The profile should include all the areas of their business, their challenges, their competition. This will help you link what you're selling to what they need.

How to identify new opportunities with existing customers

We use two methods:

- Profiling existing customers (or re-profiling, if things have changed for them)
- Creating a product matrix

Profiling your customers

For us, profiling means "Understanding everything about your client's business in order to uncover opportunities to sell."

The best way to build a profile of a customer is to start with how their company earns its revenue, and work backwards, looking at every angle where your product or service might fit in. This means that you're looking at new data and new information in relation to what they sell, who they sell to, how they sell it, how they produce it, their suppliers, the back office mechanisms – every aspect of their business. From this you'll get some ideas on where your products or services can fit in.

Creating a product matrix

This is a fun, nerdy thing to do that puts an overview and structure into finding new opportunities with existing customers. Put your results from your profiling into your matrix.

Simply list your products across the top of a Microsoft Excel spreadsheet or similar tool, and your existing customers down the left-hand side, like this:

CUSTOMER	PRODUCT				
	A	B	C	D	E
ABC Company	N	O	A	?	?
DEF Company	O	?	?	N	A
GHI Corporation	?	?	N	A	O
JKL Enterprises	A	N	?	A	O
XYZ Builders	?	A	O	?	N

LABEL DESCRIPTION: A - We have all the business, O - there is an Opportunity here, N - They do not need, ? - I don't need and need to find out

Figure 2

Decide descriptors for the relationship between your products and your clients. We use:

- A: We have all of the business. Yay, us!
- O: We've spotted an opportunity.
- N: No opportunities. And, yes, we've checked.
- I: Might be opportunities. Needs investigation.

When you first do this, you might end up with a spreadsheet full of question marks, because you don't know all the answers. List the actions to take or questions to ask next time you visit your customers.

Peter's story: How the product matrix works in action

I sat down with a salesperson and we put together their product matrix. We had little information and ended up with 32 question marks in the matrix. Two months later we met again. The salesperson had undertaken 22 meetings with existing clients – and these were not extra meetings, just ones that were scheduled anyway. Through finding out more and questioning their clients, the salesperson had added 18 opportunities to their pipeline and had already closed 8 deals worth 56,000 USD and around 88,000 USD in the pipeline. They thought it was a useful exercise.

Some straws: Selling to existing customers

- Profile or reprofile all your tier one clients at least annually.
- Build a product matrix and review it monthly. Add actions from it to your sales activity task list.
- Check that you're managing all the opportunities in your pipeline.

Putting up the prices

Once you've made a sale, one thing happens. And that's time. After a while, you may need, or be forced, to put the prices up. You may also want to put your prices up because it's one of the easiest ways to increase your profitability.

How you approach putting the price up makes a huge difference in how it's received by your customer, and how (or if) it's accepted.

Why it's important to put the price up

Your company might be excellent at driving down costs, but this could be because it feels so much easier to squeeze more out of suppliers and staff. But who benefits from your cost and efficiency efforts? Your existing customers, that's who. In our experience, companies tend to maintain or improve their profitability through cost control, rather than increasing their revenue through putting up their prices. And that's because they're scared of doing so.

This is understandable, because who wants to give out bad news? But let's take a look at the numbers. Putting up your prices can have a massive positive impact on your profit. Here are some numbers we prepared earlier:

	Current	After 5% Increase	Difference, $	Difference, %
Annual Turnover	10,000,00	10,500,00	500,000	5%
Profit	1,000,000	1,500,000	500,000	50%

In this example, a 5% increase in revenue, delivers a 50% increase in profit. That's tasty.

You can see that a relatively modest price increase has a considerable impact on profit. There's always a risk that you may lose customers, so it's not something to be approached without careful consideration and planning.

Salespeople often fight against price rises because they're the ones that have to implement it, and it's not easy. It's inherently bad news for the customer.

How to approach price rises

First, it's important that you have a strategy. The drive for a price increase should come from the sales leadership team and company's senior management. It can't be the decision of a lone salesperson because, to be credible, it needs corporate clout behind it.

It's important that salespeople should be supported and prepared by your sales leaders, so:

- Prepare your sales team fully and include them in the strategy and planning for price increases.
- Make sure that the sales team fully understands the importance and impact of putting prices up.
- Establish clear rules and guidelines on which clients will have the price increases, and which won't. You may like to exempt some of your customers, for different reasons.
- Incentivise your sales team for getting increases.

Putting up the prices: a strategy

1. Set up a meeting with your sales team

Brainstorm ways to justify the price increase by:

- Considering the likely objections.
- Thinking through the value you're still giving your clients.

It's super-important to prepare justification for price rises. Don't forget to develop reasons for meeting customers other than to simply discuss the price increase.

2. Prepare a price increase letter

Spend time drafting a letter that accompanies your visit to cover the price increase. Although you don't want to make it a big deal, you do need to formalise it. The letter should be brief but carefully worded, making it clear that you appreciate their custom.

3. Visit your customers with the letter

Unless they are a low-value customer, don't just send the price increase letter, or email if you don't need to be too official, but combine it with a visit. Try to ensure that you have some other news (preferably good) for them, that will be of real interest. There must be something that's new at your company that will impress your contact. Don't just turn up with news of the price increase, as it will quickly become pretty awkward. Have the price increase as a side issue.

Although the price increase won't be the only reason for your visit, ensure that you're clear about the subject. Don't half-heartedly leave the letter on the desk and run. If you yourself believe that the increase is justified, you'll appear more confident.

4. Follow up your visit

After your meeting, you won't always know how successful you have been with your price increase. Is the customer looking at alternatives? Or have they fully accepted the increase? Getting answers to these questions may be difficult as if you call the customer and ask, "Is everything OK with the price hike?", there's a risk that this will re-open the discussion and make them believe that there's still room for negotiation. If you don't stay in contact though, they may be looking elsewhere, and you won't find out until they stop buying from you.

So, we've found that making another appointment two or three weeks after the price increase visit can confirm it for you. Bring something useful to the visit, then at the end of the meeting ask something like, "Have you heard much from the competition recently?" Often the way your client responds will let you know if the matter is closed, or if they've been looking at other options. If they're not looking, then they won't link your question to the price increase.

One thing to always remember when discussing a price increase is that your customers are probably having the same discussions with their own clients.

Peter's story: If you don't ask, you don't get

Sometimes price increases aren't scary. A salesperson I managed was scared of losing business when it came to increasing prices. He spent more time trying to persuade me not to increase the price than persuading the customers to accept it. Together we developed a plan for him to start to tackle the issue, and he put it into practice. It didn't work with all his clients, but the majority accepted the increase during the introductory stage of the plan. They were pretty much expecting a price increase, and all we did was lean on an open door. Panic over for the salesperson. It was an easy task and the outcome was a lot of extra profit. Sorted.

Some straws: Putting up the prices

- Include price increases as part of your sales strategy.
- Make sure you create some strong justification to help your clients accept it.
- If you've prepared well, you will feel more confident.

CHAPTER 16:
Managing existing customers

What's this about?

Your existing customers are a great source of sales and that's why it's important to know how to manage them. In this section you'll find out how to decide which customers you can and should spend more time on, and which you can keep warm. You'll learn why a customer management strategy is your key tool to manage your existing customers properly.

Managing your existing customers is important because:

- You need to protect your business from your competition.
- There's always potential for more sales within your existing clients.
- It's an easier way to grow revenue.
- It costs less and helps you achieve your targets more easily.
- It makes chasing new business less critical.

- Lost business almost always has a negative impact on company results.

Very often, existing customers are neglected because businesses focus most of their selling efforts on winning new business from new customers. But your existing customers are arguably your most valuable ones. This is because it costs less and is significantly more profitable to maintain an existing customer than it is to keep losing business and then having to win additional new customers to make up for the shortfall.

The key to managing existing customers is to strike a balance between good customer service, where you check that your customers are happy with what they've bought, and good salespersonship, where you identify and follow opportunities for more business.

In order to protect your clients from the competition, follow the three rules of customer management: relationship, relationship, relationship. Protecting your customers from the competition is called 'brickwalling', because you're building a metaphorical brick wall around your customer, so that they're not interested in your competition, and your competition cannot get to them.

Please, please do not build a literal brick wall around your clients. This never works.

You don't want your metaphorical brick wall to stifle your client, but to grow them, too.

OK, maybe a greenhouse might be a better metaphor. Build a greenhouse round your client. The bugs/competition can't get to them but you can give them all the water and nutrition they need to blossom i.e. buy your stuff.

I think we're done with the metaphors for this section.

Customer management strategy

What's customer management strategy?

Customer management strategy is the process you use to enable you to look after your customers to achieve your objectives. It's how you plan, organise and take action. And, of course, customer management isn't always about customers – every sector is different. For instance, in the construction industry, you may need to nurture more people than your direct client; for instance the architects, consultants or end user.

Why is having a strategy important?

Being strategic about managing your customers means that you'll do more of the right things at the right time with the right customers. You'll spend more of your effort on the things that get the most rewards, but you'll also not miss out on opportunities. Having a strategy means that you're taking a consistent approach to nurturing your customers. Being consistent pays off.

Developing a structure for your strategy

You're looking to create a system of relationship assessment that allows you to look at all key points that matter to your clients, and then measuring yourself against targets set against each key point.

You may like to head up your strategy with activities that might produce results, for instance:

- Meeting more contacts.
- Understanding more about their business.
- Educating them on different aspects of our products.
- Involving them in a charitable activity.
- Showing gratitude for their business.

To choose what you want to measure, decide on your goals. Maybe it's to maximise your revenue from each client within a year. Think to yourself, "What needs to happen for me to be in this position this time next year?"

One simple measurable exercise may be around direct contact with a particular person at a client: Think through:

- How often should you meet face-to-face?
- How often should you invite them for hospitality?
- How often should you phone or message them?
- Have you sent them monthly updates?
- Have you presented all of your products to them in the last 12 months?
- Have you held a Lunch'n'Learn for them and their team?
- Have you met the senior management?

- Have they met your senior management?

For different customers the numbers and activities may differ, but the key point is to decide what's important and then add it into your strategy.

From your activity list, create a strategy sheet like this one:

CUSTOMER PRODUCT		
Activity	Question	Yes/No
Hospitality	Have we completed any hospitality in the last 12 months?	
Regular Visits	Have we been visiting the client on a monthly basis for the last 3 months?	
Project Pipeline	Am I aware of their Project Pipeline?	
Educate	Are we happy the client is aware of all our products and strenghts?	
Senior Visit	Has a senior manager visited them in the past 3 months?	
Contacts	Am I happy I have a healthy relationship with all of the key contacts?	

If you spend half an hour reviewing this once a month, it'll tell you what you should be doing next with each client.

Some straws: Customer management strategy

- Put your strategic review time in your CRM or task list or whatever system you use to manage your sales activity.
- Add strategic tasks to your CRM, so you'll get reminders about what you should be doing each day.

- Don't take for granted long-term or regular customers. If you neglect them, or put them at the bottom of your To Nurture list, they'll jump ship if someone shinier comes along.

Segmenting your customers

You might have thought to yourself: "But if I look after every single customer the same, I literally have no time to eat, sleep and be a human."

Don't worry, the sales industry has thought of this. The key to managing your energy and efforts when you're looking after your existing clients is segmentation.

What's customer segmentation?

Segmenting your customers is dividing your existing customers into particular groups, and assigning each group with a level of time and effort. This helps you spend the right amount of time, energy and focus on doing the right thing with the right customers, in a structured manner.

Why is customer segmentation important?

Every customer is different. Some clients are more profitable, or you value them more than others for whatever reason is appropriate to your business. But, at the same time, you don't want to neglect any client, because you need to protect the business you have with them. Your time is limited, so it makes sense to create a strategy to manage all your customers effectively. And that's through customer segmentation.

How to segment your customers in four simple steps:

1. Decide on the criteria for segmentation, and make it measurable.
2. Decide how many segments (we call them tiers) you need.
3. Decide on your plan for each tier.
4. Pop your customers into the right tier, depending on how they measure up against the criteria in step one.

About tiers

Customer segmentation avoids the difficulties of creating a management plan for every single customer. Instead, you create tiers, and create a plan for each tier. Then you pop each of your clients into a tier and manage them according to your plan for that tier.

How many tiers you create depends on the nature of your business and the market but it's best to keep it simple. In our experience, three tiers is a sensible number.

The customers you drop into the highest tier should be those who are most valuable to you, now and in the future. They need most of your effort. Your second tier is important and needs dedicated time. Your third tier needs some love and affection, but might just be keeping them warm with some low-effort information they'd find interesting.

What criteria for segmentation should you use?

Segmentation criteria will depend on what's important to your business. Usually profitability and revenue is a major consideration. So, criteria for segmentation could include:

- The current revenue you receive from the customer.
- The potential revenue you could receive.
- The level of profitability each customer is contributing.
- Their payment history.
- How they are placed in their industry e.g. their strategic partners.

Customer A Billed $ 50,000 last year. This was 50% growth on the year before as they are new in the market. You have all their business, but the growth rate is expected to continue as a result of their own performance. They use a wide range of all your products and services which are all profitable.
Customer B Billed $90,000 last year. They billed $110,000 the year before and this trend has continued over the last few years. You are aware they spend $40,000 with your competition. They use a variety of your products / services, and all are profitable.
Customer C Billed $30,000 last year. This was the first year they have been a client of yours and you are aware they are spending $115,000 with your competitors. They are using a product of yours which is extremely profitable.
Customer D Billed $80,000 last year. They have been a client of yours for many years now. You have all of their business, but they are executing some expansion plans that could have a very positive impact on your business with them. They are using a product of yours which is not very profitable.

Try this exercise for size. Which of these customers deserves more of your sales team's time?

Did you find this difficult? If you did, that's the right answer, because it **is** difficult. All four customers deserve similar attention and would therefore fall into the same tier but for different reasons. The goal of putting effort into prioritising your customers is to put them into the correct category so that you can then set a plan to manage that category going forward.

A plan for each tier

Here's what to consider when creating your plan for each tier:

- How regular should contact be? A higher tier customer may well have weekly visits whereas a customer in a lower tier may receive quarterly visits with monthly phone calls. You need to decide how best you can hold on to their business without it being a huge cost to your organisation.
- Should you offer hospitality, and, if so, what kind? What would be appropriate?
- How many contacts should you have within each customer organisation? Higher tier customers will require multiple contacts across various functions than those in a lower tier.
- Should you be the only contact with your customer, or would it be useful to build relationships between their functional departments, and yours? How far can you integrate?

- Can you offer additional value, such as specialist software, training or logistics? If so, to whom should you offer it?

A straw: Segmenting customers

Review your customer segmentation strategy every three months. Do you still have the right client in the right tier?

Managing your contacts

Depending on how large your current contract is with your existing clients, you might stay in contact with more than one person in your client's company. You've already met the decision maker, but, to manage an existing customer well, you need to know how to identify and manage all the other key contacts.

Why is this important?

Overall, managing your contacts correctly is important because contacts help you give better service to your existing customers, and that means more business for you. But there's more. Managing your contacts is important because:

It would be weird and illegal to camp out at our customers' premises 24/7 and listen to their discussions. But we need to find out what's going on that affects us. Decisions are being made all of the time without our knowing. The more of the right people we know, the more these types of decisions will go our way.

- If you know more people, you'll also be able to gain more understanding about your client, and spot more opportunities to add value and sell.
- Different contacts help you with different goals. Different people in your client's organisation are valuable for:
  - Helping you understand their business and how your product or service is used.
  - Getting deals over the line.
  - Being paid on time.
  - Understanding the strategy picture.
  - General support.

How to manage your clients well

It makes sense to be organised, because you'll have a lot of contacts across all your client organisations. If you have a CRM system, all well and good. If you don't, it's time to create one.

Here's a very simple way of arranging your customer contacts for each organisation in each of your customer tiers:

Company Name	

CONTACT				
Designation	Relevance	Name	Contact Number	Current Relationship

This is what it means:

Designation: This is the role of the person. Sometimes you may not know a name, but you know a role that you want to create a relationship with, say, for instance, the head of buying in a different location of your current contact.

Relevance: Is the relationship where it should be? What is its quality?

Name/Contact Number: Here's where you put their name and contact information. Easy!

Current relationship: Honesty is good. If you messed up with the last meeting, jot down what happened and how you need to make it right. You want to make sure that all your relationships are where you want them to be, and to keep creating activities to get you there. Keep working on relationship quality.

How to get access to people you don't know yet

The best way of contacting new people is to ask for an introduction through your existing contact. Remember, it's ok to ask for referrals! It won't upset your relationship with them, if you give them a reason that will encourage and motivate them to make the introduction.

Peter's story: The danger of being too relaxed

I was managing a salesperson that had a great relationship with the person using the service that we had sold to the customer organisation. He invited them to a lot of hospitality but, out of nowhere, we lost the business. When my salesperson went to see their contact, they were told that their boss (who we never knew) had met with a competitor and been given a better offer. She fought for us but lost. We were too relaxed with the existing contact and, as a result. had never even tried to ask for an introduction to her boss.

A straw: Managing your contacts

Take some time to review each of your customers. With the knowledge you have, identify the people or roles who might be useful to you — and to whom you might add value — and build a structure on how you can meet and build relations with them.

Conclusion

Being in sales is not an easy job. We appreciate that it's hard to get everything right, all of the time. And we know that sometimes it can feel overwhelming to know where to start, to start to make a difference.

But we hope that this book has given you some tools and encouragement to start that process. It only takes a few straws to add up, until, suddenly, you'll get a breakthrough. Practice really does make a difference. By working on small things consistently, by tweaking your own attitude, you'll get where you want to be.

Stay focussed. Stick with the fundamentals. Make lots of rain. Make lots of sales.